Consciously Creating Camelot

The Body's Journey to Immortality

and the

Birth of the Divine Human

Kathy Dobson

Book design by LaVidaCo Communications

Printed in the United States of America

Library of Congress Control Number: 2019936499

ISBN 978-1-950419-01-2

"Don't let it be forgot
That once there was a spot
For one brief shining moment
That was known as Camelot..."

Table of Contents

Dedicated to...

Mom and Dad, who taught me the true meaning of Love through example, and gave me room to explore and discover for myself my own path to Divinity.

To Barb and Kerry Jean. Two hearts joined as one.

And, to all who seek Truth in the innocence of Love and the Masters of Light who so generously support me on this journey with their love, strength, and inspiration. Gently but firmly you guide me, keeping me on the path. You are loved.

Preface

I cannot be authentic about the teachings in this book without being authentic about their source.

With immense gratitude and love in my heart I honor the energies of Merlin, the Master Magician, Alchemist and *wickedly wonderful Wizard* whose magical energies once again ignite and fill the air with excitement about the unfolding of the New Golden Age of Mankind, the New Camelot.

Yes, I am talking Merlin of old; the great Alchemist, Wise Wizard and Master Magician who has been eagerly waiting for these times to unfold when once again magic rules the hearts of men.

For me, the energies of Merlin began coming through to my conscious understanding after the transition of my parents in 2012. They passed within 6 weeks of one another after 67 years together and no doubt this opened within me a floodgate of energetic consciousness patterns that needed adjusting and transmuting to higher energy. It was a serious clearing, cleansing and portal opening.

This is when I began to pick up on the energies and understand the message of Merlin. Not only was Merlin coming through in wise teachings, (i.e., Miriandra Rota's channeling of Merlin and other sources), but Camelot was showing up in my life everywhere. My dad had given my mom a music box with Camelot as the theme music. I don't ever remember seeing it before, but it ended up in my hands at the same time as Merlin's energy came shining through. This is when the title of this book was revealed to me. I just didn't realize it at the time.

Another rather interesting and fun note happened the morning that Merlin came through in his intensity, I knew and felt the energies "without doubt" ...it was that powerful. When stepping outside that morning to greet the "Sun" – to greet Sol/Ra – it was as though I was floating on air...I knew that something intense has happened, had opened and connected me with Merlin and his loving and magical energies.

But even I was not braced for what I "saw" next. After doing a bit of a spin about in the driveway with this incredible energy flowing through me, I was stunned as I stared back at my house.

Directly – and I mean directly – over my house was a rainbow, a very clear and distinct rainbow that seemed to run from my neighbor's yard a short distance away right over my house and down. It was 7 in the morning.

I was stunned and immediately ran and got my camera

and managed to capture the moment as well as I could. As you can see from the pic the rainbow wraps right over my house. There were only a few clouds in the sky that morning; it was basically clear and dry out...except over my roof where a few clouds had gathered to create this improbable rainbow. (In color, the background is clear blue sky. The only clouds in the sky were directly over my home.)

Now, you could call all this coincidence, and there are those who would; however, I believe anyone reading these words is high enough in conscious understanding that they are fully aware there are no coincidences in life, and that everything contains a message for those who are awake and aware with "eyes that see and ears that hear."

Merlin is real, and his energies are a vibration that you tap into by raising your own vibration, by resonating with it. Anyone can raise their vibration to match these energies with the intent of the heart to do so. I highly recommend it.

Love is always available to those reaching for it, and there are none so willing to give it and receive it than the

Masters who serve us from higher realms; those great and mighty ones that have traveled this road before us and mastered their own challenges and opportunities.

Merlin is a Master Alchemist, *an expert in the transformation and transmutation of energies,* and a teacher of great Light and Love. His energy archetype is one of magic, awe, and wonder. He is a great Avatar of this new dispensation, this New Camelot emerging.

His teachings are simple and full of joy, laughter, excitement, and discovery...all these define the Merlin energies. He has a great sense of humor, loves to make you laugh, and makes studying Truth fun.

When these teachings began coming through with such clarity, I was completely absorbed in the simplicity of them. Merlin seems to have a way of cutting through all the "red tape" right to the *heart* of the matter, but in a most fun, playful, and simple manner. You just want to hang out with him and learn from him.

Even a child can understand what Merlin teaches as it is all about intended Love and our understanding and clear expression of this magical essence. It's about living and expressing as a child again...innocent, connected, and authentic.

That's what the New Camelot is all about. The veils are being lifted from our understanding and clarity of Truth/ Love, and its radiant simplicity is left shining as a perfect diamond...without distortion or flaws.

There are many Light-workers who are resonating,

connecting with, and bringing forth Merlin's powerful archetypal energy in these expansive, accelerated Light-filled times – the glorious birth of the New Camelot. My heart overflows with gratitude to count myself among them. To be able to share these expansive consciousness teachings with you are a joy and a fulfillment of my heart that words alone cannot express.

These empowering teachings are not meant for me alone; they have a vibration attached to them, as everything does, and are meant for anyone whose heart resonates, whose heart is ready to accept and embrace them, whose heart is ready to live them. I joyfully hear them, follow them, and share them. *It is my honor to do so.*

Merlin's energy is the energy of "now," of focus and intent in the present moment. His teachings are all about the transformation and transmutation of energy using the power of our conscious, directed, and focused Love in the present moment, where action and magic are performed.

Merlin, the wisest and most playful of Teachers, has been a great comfort and joy to me, and I remain a loyal servant to his loving message.

In service to Love,

Kathy

....

"You are becoming conscious of this journey and, my dears, when you are conscious of something, you can directly participate! Perhaps you would receive that last statement again."

– Merlin

Acknowledgments

Much gratitude to friends and family members for their support, patience, encouragement and just plain love and time as I grew into these teachings. And to Jo-Ann Langseth for her expert editing.

To Susan Fontana who has been my spiritual partner throughout this adventure and with whom I shared one of my greatest moments upon this earth. I am forever grateful for your patience, authentic love and beaming white light. Thanks for sharing this euphoric ride with me!

To Shailaa and William Stillwater for being my ultimate cheerleaders, supporters and unending source of enlightened material. To Dr. Janni Lloyd, Christina Mickel and Debbie Hart for being my "eyes and ears" before publishing and to all members of our Physically Immortal FB Group for igniting my passion to get this published!

   With love to David LaGesse and Laura Stanton at LaVidaCo Communications for their invaluable and generous hard work and focused time and attention in getting the book content laid out and cover created and ready for publication. It's been waiting for your touch.

   To Miriandra Rota whose channelings of Merlin inspired these wonderful Truth teachings to come forth.

   And, foremost, to beloved Master Merlin...

Introduction

This book is about play and magic, the same magic that is performed in the chrysalis of a caterpillar. It's the magic of creation. Even more...*it is the magic of conscious creation!*

This book is about expanding consciousness; it is about the practice of expanding consciousness. Are you ready for change? Do you feel this shift?

It is about releasing the old patterns of how to live, and creating and embracing the new expanded versions of Love.

And, it starts and ends with you.

There is a new way of living and *knowing*, of creating and participating with LIFE, with Love, as it expands its awareness through every adventure and experience – without the fear and resistance of condemnation, judgment, and boundaries.

This book is about the butterfly that emerges when we let go of the caterpillar. When we surrender our personal opinionated world and open our wings to a new world of expansive Love, we fly free. Replacing the oppressive prison of fear is Love of life, of discovery and journeying, and experiencing *with the freedom, wonder, and awe of a child.*

The caterpillar could never become a butterfly if it did not flow with life and follow its inner urge to be more, to experience more. And it does so with full faith and acceptance, without resistance.

It is time for the butterfly within you to crack open your chrysalis and emerge. What started out as a comfortable place to transform is now the only thing between you and freedom.

This is your new story if you are willing to let go and open your heart widely to Love *as it expresses now,* in its ever-expanding journey into manifestation. Come, journey forth with me in discovery mode, full of wonder, awe, and excitement. Come and play in the ever-present moment where All Possibility exists to express JOY *eternally.*

This is an adventure you will never forget as you become a conscious creator, participating in the gloriously eternal dance of life without resistance. You'll spread your butterfly wings and soar to heights previously unimagined. You'll know freedom as never before.

You are becoming an *empowered Cosmic Butterfly in the Land of Camelot.*

Kathy Dobson
February, 2019

The Truth

You lose your mind in the past of your life, you lose your mind in the future of your life...but you gain your mind in the Present of your life.

1

One Heart, One Mind

There isn't a day that one of us does not wake up. If you are reading this, it means you wake every day, just as I do.

But, the question is, how do you start and end your day? Do you begin and end in the power of Love? Are you able to remain peaceful and emotionally balanced no matter what comes your way?

Most people, if being *totally honest,* would answer "no" to that question.

This little gem has come to your rescue. It's going to take you by the hand and give you the tools, knowledge, powerful insights, and inspiration to stay grounded in Love, from the moment you wake in the morning till you lay your head down at night to enter and play in higher realms.

It will reveal to you the newly recognized Divine System for living and manifesting...*without thinking.* It will introduce you to *magic.*

This system of living and creating has been secreted for thousands of years, and as we begin our entrance into the Golden Age of Mankind, the time has come for the consciousness of mankind to *understand and use with clarity these advanced laws.*

My own journey into this realm of magic did not happen overnight. It comes through firsthand experience. Over 40 years ago, I had a major awakening, a *lightning bolt* of clarity that shifted my own conscious understanding and suddenly "I had eyes that could see and ears that could hear." I seemed to know and understand a higher purpose behind all things, and I've been on a Truth - revealing mission ever since. It includes lots of study, meditation, discovery, research, insights, and ongoing enlightenment.

I've lived, loved, cried, and laughed through it all and I am here to shorten your path, to make your "yoke light and your burden easy," if you will let me. I've cut through many brambles along the way that will help ease your own transition...but you must listen and adjust your perceptions and *leave all contaminated thoughts behind.*

Did I mention struggle? Yep, lots of that too. And that is precisely why I am here: to take you out of struggle, to show you that there is a new way to live, different from how you are experiencing life now. It is a life without struggle!

Life is not a chore! It is a *Joy,* and I guarantee you that by the time you finish reading this book you too will know what it is you need to do, say, and be to stay anchored in Love throughout every experience you encounter.

It is as simple as child's play because it is child's play.

Love is so much bigger than our present perceptions allow us to understand. So, the first prerequisite to moving on in this book is an OPEN MIND. Remain in your dead thoughts and I can't reach you...and neither will anyone else.

Close your mind and you learn nothing new. Open your mind and watch the wonder!

The old ways aren't working as they seemed to in the past; they don't resonate with this new energy, this vibration/ frequency, this expanded Truth/Love energy revealing itself.

Keep in mind that Love is eternal, just as Truth is eternal. They are one and the same. Even beyond the clarity and understanding of Love that is being revealed to us now are dimensions of Love we will continue to move into, *eternally.*

Open the door of your mind to instruction in a new way of living, of aligning with a dawning *consciousness of Love.* Tune in to this energy by letting go of your personal world... your preconceived ideas (your resistance) of how life should or should not be, allowing this new energy to take residence. Tune in, as you would a radio. It's that simple.

This new energy is the magic, and once you connect with it, creating is easy!

However, you cannot tune in to the expanded Love channel until you've cleared your other channels. You must *tune out* of lower-frequency channels to tune in to the higher-frequency channel of expanding Love consciousness. As with a stereo system, you cannot give attention to two channels at once without utter confusion.

"Ye cannot drink the Cup of the LORD, and the Cup of Devils: Ye cannot be partakers of the LORD'S Table, and of the Table of Devils!"   —*(1st Corinthians 10:21)*

The "Cup of the LORD" is Love and the Cup of Devils is *all thoughts outside of Love.*

This book is about removing the static and living the magic.

This is the new world/playground we're consciously moving into. It's a world of magic, and the only requirement for living and playing in this realm is that *you must become as children again to enter through these gates.*

There is a sign on the playground gate, and it reads:

PLAYGROUND OF THE YOUniverse
Only innocent children allowed.
All problems must be left at the gate.
No baggage allowed in.
Leave excess weight behind.

No anger, hate, jealousy, fear, guilt, greed, chaos, resentment, sadness, depression, disorder, frowns, pride, or any of their resonating, clamoring cousins allowed in.

No preconceived ideas, no judgments, no condemnations or criticisms, no opinions about others or self, no doubts or resistance, no fears about the future or regrets about the past. These all must be cleared out and left at the entrance. No karma, no past and future, no limits, borders, boundaries, negative thoughts, feelings or emotions are allowed in.

Only love, joy, harmony, praise, gratitude, giving, sharing, allowing, believing, laughter, appreciation, surrender, confidence, courage, inspiration, smiles and service are allowed in this beautiful playground.

Power, clarity, ease, order, justice, understanding, acceptance, empathy, imagining without boundaries or conditions, innocence, trust, compassion, passion, exploration, journeying, adventure – you'll find all of that here.

Love, Truth, Wisdom, Empowerment, Peace, Presence, Joy, Harmony, Abundance, Creativity, Imagination, Excitement, Discovery, Serendipity, Synchronicity, Spontaneity, Balance, Health, Authenticity, Choice, Action, Freedom, Eternity, Miracles and Magic are just some of the main attractions!

The moment, the present, the "now" is your experience on this playground, where you continually feel the excitement of the "moment" *because there is no past or future here. There is only the "present," the gift that life gives us eternally. That is all there is.*

You are now in the "flow" and aligned with the frequency of Love, your true authentic self – the playground without limits. *Go forth, frolic, and play for eternity.*

....

Eternity is the moment, the land of the living,
the land of Love.

....

The Energy

"If you wish to understand the Universe, think of energy, frequency and vibration."

- Nikola Tesla

2

Shifty Dimensions

Unless you've been living in a cave these past few years, you've likely heard or read something about this "shift" we're presently experiencing. Although most people have heard about it, they are still clueless as to what it is or what is happening because of it.

You cannot really understand the shift until you start thinking in terms of energy/consciousness, vibrations, frequency, awareness, densities, and dimensions. All these terms define and measure the amount of light flowing.

This shift is an energy shift, a *frequency shift in consciousness.* (Everything is a form of energy and an expression of energy, and this is one basic scientific principle you must understand – everything vibrates.)

Consciousness – our energy signature – is shifting to a faster frequency, a different dimension of perception, an expanded, Divine way of thinking, creating and living.

As multidimensional beings (able to be conscious of multiple dimensions at once), our level of thought defines the level of consciousness we presently dwell in. Since consciousness is fluid, we are continually shifting from one dimension to another depending on our focus, attention, and perceptions – our level of awareness.

Each state of consciousness or density of awareness has its own corresponding characteristics or ways of thinking, feeling and expressing…its own laws and principles specific to that level of energetic frequency. Each level gets more fluidly free (vibrating faster) as it progresses to the next.

We are currently advancing from the 3rd and 4th dimensions (the 3rd density) of conscious understanding to the 5th dimension (the 4th density) of conscious understanding and expression.

Understanding and expression of what, you ask? Love. Love is the energy of the Universe.

Love is all there is when you begin to perceive creation from a singular point of view. It has always been about Love, for Love is Source energy and the only reality there is. It's where the magic is.

"Love is the energy of life." …Robert Browning

Remember, consciousness is fluid and the level of your thoughts defines the level of consciousness that you operate from. Some people spend a great deal of time in the higher dimension of Love while others spend most of their time in the lower frequency of fear.

The densest conscious thinking is focused solely on the physical world and locked in a time/space and cause/effect paradigm. Rules and restrictions, borders, barriers and limits all live here. Those who constantly feel victimized by outside influences (finger points out all the time) are entrenched here where life feeds them everything they need to feel more of the same. They believe they are separate from everyone and everything else.

Their world is an ever-dueling world of good and bad, of opposing forces at battle in their mind – an angel on one shoulder and a devil on the other. Living in fear, they play the victim role, and all things outside of themselves become suspect because they don't see the Unity, the Oneness, the Single Source of Love.

Rigid with rules and structures and home to duality/polarity – the "cause and effect" of things – this low-density consciousness level is the realm of fear and survival where "if this is so, then that is the result" thinking dictates action. Work and toil are mandatory and expected here, as victims continually create dramas to fill with energy. Fear rules, duality is the name of the game, and karma is born and thrives. (This is our existence, after eating from the Tree of the Knowledge of "good and evil," and leaving Unity consciousness.)

In this lower state of consciousness, we are powerless and have not yet discovered who we are. Our vision is narrow, and we only see and participate with the world outside of us, the world of our physical senses. Everything in this world is transitory, temporary and fleeting.

Fourth-dimensional consciousness is the transitional dimension or gateway between rigid 3D consciousness and fluid 5D. It is the home of the Astral Realm, the dimension we reside in when sleeping and dreaming and after we've passed-over.

We begin to take *conscious residence* in 4D when we tire of the dramas the outer world presents, seek a higher purpose in life, turn within and consciously and earnestly begin our inner journey of self-discovery – becoming aware of ourselves as being Divine in nature. We eventually come to embrace our Unity and Oneness with life, with Source (with God, or whatever title suits you), and this new perception launches us from victimhood to self-responsibility, to self-empowerment.

There is only one story being told, one play being played out, and that one is about the growth and expansion of Love and our conscious understanding and expression of this Life force energy.

Imagine the caterpillar encased within its cocoon/chrysalis silently metamorphosing from its low frequency (crawling/slow/dense/limited) to a high frequency (flying/fast/light/free).

Our dense physical bodies cannot sustain 5D vibrations without transitioning any more than a mineral can sustain itself as a plant or a plant can sustain itself as an animal without acquiring the new physical properties needed for life in their new realm.

We, as consciousness expressing in form, acquire new bodies/new properties to take us into and sustain us in each dimension, and the shift to 5D is no different. Our atomic body structure is evolving from our present lower-vibrational, carbon-based structure to a higher-frequency silica/crystalline-based one. It is changing/evolving from dark, dense carbon into *free-flowing Light, just as a caterpillar changes into a "butterfly of f-light."*

Sounds like fun, doesn't it?

To understand better, just imagine yourself at the subatomic level, where frequency and vibration are obvious to your logic. This is the level that you are changed at...your inner quantum level where your frequency expresses. When your frequency shifts at the quantum level *where the controls are*, your outer expression changes as your whole-body structure and life change to reflect the inner; they are connected. One is but a reflection of the other.

Each frequency expansion bears its own unique characteristics and offers a plethora of learning opportunities that contribute to the evolution of both the spiritual and physical realms. This shift concerns conscious awakening/self-awareness. *Consciousness is becoming aware of itself – i.e., awareness is moving to a higher and deeper understanding of itself.*

As the new self-awareness is awakened, the old is transformed until we reach a state at which we can "consciously with intent know and express ourselves as Love," our true authentic selves.

From a consciousness point of view, *dimensional shifts are all about the ever-expanding awareness of our understanding and expression of Love, for Love is all there is...it is Light and Life.*

As the passageway or "rainbow bridge" to higher-frequency dimensions, think of the 4th dimension as the wash-and-rinse cycle, cleansing our present dual mind for entrance into higher dimensions of Unity consciousness. Among other things, it is our clearing and prep zone of consciousness. You simply cannot take lower frequency thoughts into the high, finer frequency of the 5th dimension. They don't resonate, *they must go; they are the very things that are keeping you out of the 5th dimension.*

Although still under the influence of "cause and effect" (past-and-future mentality), 4D is more fluid than 3D and helps loosen our "death" grip on duality. We begin to let go and allow a more fluid level of conscious understanding to take root and grow on our way to 5D, the dimension of Eternity," where there is no time as we know it. There is no past or future in this expansive dimension where we experience more levels of awareness while continuing to master love, light and life (love and light combined). *There is only "now" the "present" moment.*

The 5th dimension is the home of Unity consciousness, where cause and effect no longer resonate. (*When you are in Unity, what is there to be the cause and effect of?*) It's where we begin our adjustment to a new way of creating and manifesting within Unity consciousness, without work, without the dueling "cause and effect," "past and future," and "good and bad," the titles and labels of things.

Those are the old ways, the ways of work and toil, the ways we are leaving behind. Work and toil produce more work and belong to one world, whereas play and magic produce miracles and belong to another.

The world you see about you is not a *cause*, it is an *effect* of consciousness. Those with 5D consciousness view the world much differently, experiencing different perceptions and perspectives from those with 3D and 4D awareness.

Someday soon, the effects we see in the world will reflect cosmic consciousness, the realm of 5D thinkers. It's called Heaven on Earth, the Golden Age of Mankind – the New Camelot.

To make things a bit clearer, imagine the dimensions this way (you'll easily see how you move from solid to transformational into Light essence).

The life of the always hungry caterpillar is our 3D world. Not so much fun, lots of work, and almost continuous striving to get to where and what we seem to need. We eventually get there, but it takes time and tremendous effort. Sometimes because life moves so slow at this density level, we never make it.

This level is very disempowering because we believe outside influences can affect our lives. We perceive ourselves as victims and can't see the expanse and possibilities of the open sky above. We live in fear, give our power away, and wear disguises to hide the truth of who we are…just as some caterpillars use mimicry to *blend in and avoid being discovered.*

Imagine the chrysalis as our 4D world. The caterpillar is transforming from a lower form into a higher form and is no longer focused on the outer world. Its reality is totally focused on the inner world, and transformation of the lower, dense energy into lighter, faster-vibrating energy. Not by destruction of lower energy (physics will tell you that you can neither create nor destroy energy; you can only witness its transformation into something new), but by *transmutation* of lower energy into higher-vibrating energy; slow frequency into fast frequency – the energy of expanded Love.

A caterpillar does not die and come back as a butterfly, it transforms while alive. Death is not involved in this process.

Did the hidden meaning of that statement unsettle you? I hope so. We are transforming into Cosmic Butterflies, and, guess what? *Physical death is not involved.* More on that subject later.

The butterfly is the 5D world. The butterfly (*that transformed but did not die*) emerges into a whole new world of freedom and creation without struggle or work. This new world is at its command as it soars above the "victims" below. It now has freedom and the ability to fly, see, explore, and discover – without limits or obstructions. It is *empowered with new perceptions, perspectives, and possibilities.*

Think about it: the world that a butterfly perceives, entertains, and expresses in is a far cry from the world a caterpillar must operate in.

You are emerging. Your glorious inner Divine Self is ready to emerge into a life free from struggle. That, I dare say, is what drew you to this book. Your real self knows magic; your real self is a Cosmic Butterfly.

The time has come in our evolutionary experience to ascend in consciousness and form to the higher dimensions, just as the caterpillar ascends from the Earth to the heavens. As grand Cosmic Butterflies, our wings have formed and we're ready to crack open our chrysalis and soar into dimensions without boundaries. We're moving out of time into Eternity and leaving fear, survival, and victimhood behind.

You may be thinking, *What? This isn't the end? There is more to life than what I presently perceive?*

Doesn't that thought feel good? Keep stretching that mind of yours! Don't let it close or you will dry up, like dust in the wind! The mind, like any other living organism, must be fed the "waters" of life if it is to stay healthy, alert, and growing (as opposed to drying up and dying).

This new time, this new era, is a new age of conscious understanding and awareness. It is a dynamic expansion of Source's understanding and expression of *Love made manifest on Earth.*

We've already established that densities and dimensions of consciousness are not really levels, not as we think of levels, but a way of expressing *where one's thinking mind is dwelling*... a way for us to understand how this energy/consciousness grows and expands in its expression of Love.

Metaphorically, levels of consciousness can be compared to the stages water can assume. When in its most dense state, it is solid, it is ice, it is cold. The vibration is very slow at this level. Heat it up a little, get those molecules moving around, and you've changed the state of ice to water, a fluid form. It is still the same substance, *but now fluid in nature.* Heat it up a bit more and the molecules are really moving, and you have steam/vapor.

Each state expresses more and more freedom. Steam is the most fluid of all these levels, just as 5D is the most fluid of all the levels of consciousness that we have experienced thus far.

Here's the analogy:

Ice/3D consciousness: that which is dense, rigid, slow, and cold; the caterpillar. The world of *conditional love*; creating karma; *it's the "you're to blame – not I" syndrome*; the finger points out. It's not surprising that we say, "He was so cold" when confronted with someone whose consciousness operates at this level. We feel this coldness... there is no warmth of Love extended.

Water/4D consciousness: much more fluid; the chrysalis of transformation. The focus has turned inward – the world of *unconditional love comes into view*; karma is cleared; birth of the *it's me – not you consciousness; I am to blame*; the finger points in.

Steam/5D consciousness: free of the constraints that ice and water are subjected to, this expansive dimension (steam) frees us from our boundaries; the butterfly. It's neither one of us; there is only One, Unity – Love. *There is no pointing, no finger, no karma, no blame.* We have developed "eyes that see and ears that hear" and wings to soar.

These boundaries we set are our own creations – our guilts, fears, judgments, and negative, distorted perceptions of life. They dam things up and slow things down to the point of being frozen. (Think Princess Elsa from the movie Frozen.)

Bestselling author Dr. Richard Gerber, in Vibrational Medicine, concludes that "All matter, including human cells, is actually frozen light."

As we absorb greater Light (more heat, more energy, more Love), our molecules and atoms vibrate quicker, and our thinking becomes more fluid (more expansive, with freedom of excitement, discovery, and participation). It is this fluidity that expands our consciousness. We move into 5D thinking, which is Unity of purpose in line with Divine Will; there are no dueling powers (polarity/cause and effect) in this world – only Unity of purpose.

To sum up, you need to understand that our consciousness levels rise as we evolve/grow in our understanding and expression of Love. Our journey from 3D to 5D takes us from the circumscribed awareness of an individual who believes that, above all, they must survive (one who is totally ruled by the outer senses/focused on the *outer world of survival; the victim*) to an awakened self-awareness of *being Divine in nature* (one who has discovered their inner world and knows of their higher, inner senses and connection to Source, to Love).

We are set to enter the Age of Aquarius, the Age of Knowledge, the Age of Knowing. The Age of *Now*. The Aquarian glyph shows water being poured from the heavens upon mankind. *Water symbolizes spirit.* The spirit of God/Source (the photons/DNA) is being poured upon our conscious understanding, raising it and expanding the expression of Love as we presently understand it.

This is a grand time indeed! *We are making a conscious evolutionary leap from one dimension to another.*

Now that we know what is shifting, let's discuss why frequencies are changing.

The Cycle of Human Consciousness

"It is a [Great] Cycle in the Sun's activity that brings in this new age. Or, more precisely, it is the passage of the Sun through other spheres of activity that creates this solar cycle."

– Edgar Cayce

3

The Great Year

Aquarius

Many of you will remember the hit song from the Musical "Hair" released in the late 60's, about the dawning of the "Age of Aquarius" by a group known as the 5th Dimension.

Even then, the Universe was giving hints of what was happening...what is happening. Although most of us listened, we never really caught what the lyrics of this song were relaying to our conscious understanding. Until now. *(Check the lyrics out online. They speak for themselves. I cannot include them here because of copyright laws.)*

We are shifting out of the Age of Pisces and into the Age of Aquarius, and this shift and rise in human consciousness is tied to *cosmic cycles* with the precession of the equinoxes as the primary player.

Cycles of Time and Our Cosmic Clock/Calendar

Nothing in the heavens sits still – everything is in motion. It is a very ordered Universe of wheels within wheels and cycles within cycles, *all focused on and defined by Light.*

Cycles are not new to us; we celebrate our lives based on cycles. We cycle through seconds, minutes, hours, days, months, and years. Although there are larger cycles in the heavens, there are three primary cycles or "wheels of time" we need be concerned with. Each cycle involves falling asleep and awakening determined by how much light is received. Two of these cycles you will recognize as the Earth day and Earth year. The other one, the Great Year, or the "cycle of precession," has not been taught to most of us.

Three Great Cycles of Earth Time:

Rotating Cycle: Day/diurnal cycle (counterclockwise rotation)

Revolving Cycle: Year (counterclockwise rotation)

Precessing Cycle: Great Year (clockwise rotation)

As the Earth spins/rotates counterclockwise on its axis, it creates a cycle we're all very familiar with called our Earth "day." We experience this 24-hour cycle as morning, noon, afternoon, and night (depending on where we are in the spin in relation to the sun). The Earth also revolves counterclockwise around the sun while it is rotating on its axis, and this creates another cycle of 12 months that defines our year. Like the daily cycle, this cycle is also defined by the light received and experienced in segments – winter, spring, summer, and fall.

Just thinking about these two cycles, day and year, makes me dizzy enough without adding in a third cycle...the *precession* cycle.

The cycle of precession is one of the longest cycles known to present-day astronomers. It concerns the tilt of the Earth's axis (where it is currently pointing) and the path of the equinoxes. This heavenly cycle moves in a clockwise motion through the zodiac, causing the constellations to move backward – thus precessing. The other two cycles, the daily cycle of the spin of the Earth and the yearly cycle of the Earth around the sun, both cycle counterclockwise.

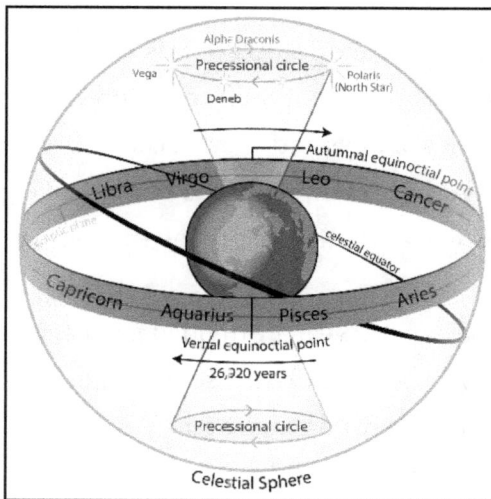

Notice the cone shape in the image above. That circle at the top is one complete *cycle of precession* as the axis of the

Earth travels around the entire zodiac. This cycle ranges from 24,000 to 25,920 years depending on the source you reference. During this journey, the axis spends approximately 2,000 plus years in each zodiac sign. To keep it simple, I will be using the number 24,000 in referencing this cycle. Consider this our great cosmic clock.

Until more recent times, the lunisolar theory (gravity from the sun and moon pulling upon the Earth) was used to explain the cycle of precession as a "wobble" of the Earth on its axis, similar to how a "top" starts to wobble as its spin slows. Although the Earth does indeed have a slight wobble, modern technology reveals that this backward movement of the constellations has more to do with the journey of our own sun, with solar system in tow, that causes the cycle of precession.

Because the cycle of precession is such a long cycle of 24,000 years, it does not get the same kind of attention that the shorter cycles of days and years receive. Obviously, none of us have lived long enough in one lifetime to experience a 24,000-year cycle, so it's not surprising that we haven't given it much thought.

Just as the day and year are divided into parts or segments all defined by how much light is received, the precession cycle is also divided and defined by how much light is received. The Greeks called these divisions of time The Ages of Man – Gold, Silver, Bronze, and Iron. The Hindus divided them into Yugas (also called Ages) – Kali, Dwapara, Treta, and Satya (or Krita), and to the Mayans, they were "worlds."

Modern science refers to this cycle as the precession of the equinoxes because it is the path of the equinoxes.

This ascending and descending cycle of precession is also expressed and known as the "Hero's Journey." Coined "the monomyth" by mythologist, author, and lecturer Joseph Campbell, it represents stages of "recurring patterns many heroes undergo over the course of their stories."

David Wilcock, best-selling author of many books including *The Synchronicity Key,* writes extensively about this cycle he calls the "Galactic Blueprint." He states, "Every myth has the hero's journey; every myth has the precession of the equinoxes mathematically hidden in it."

According to Wilcock, the cycle of precession is *"the blueprint of our soul's evolution, and the path to the Golden Age."*

The Precession Cycle, the Hero's Journey, the Platonic Year (in honor of the Greek philosopher), and the Great Year are all the same story – *the cycle of consciousness growth, or the evolution of human consciousness.*

We are shifting into a more expanded version of consciousness, a newer dimension of perception. Egyptians, Mayans, Incas, Hopis and Aztecs, among other ancient ancestors and tribes, as well as other religions and cultures worldwide, knew this and expressed it in their myths, calendars, architecture, and art. It's what all the fuss and excitement about these times is all about.

Just as we celebrate our lives with birthdays, anniversaries, centennials, bicentennials, etc., how much more does the Universe celebrate one of its own mega-milestones as the sun completes another 24,000-year cycle/orbit through the cosmos and moves back into the Light?

In this highly charged central core of the galaxy that the sun has entered and aligned us with (Mayan myths refer to this region as the "nuclear bulge"), we are entering an "interstellar cloud" (the term NASA uses), known esoterically as the Photon Belt or Manasic Ring (referring to mind). It is an intense region of gamma rays, photonic energy transmissions, the most energetic form of light.

This highly charged interstellar cloud is a ring of energy shaped like a donut standing on its side. Alcyone, the primary super-star of the Pleiades Constellation, is always within this circle of intense light often referred to as the "rings of Alcyone." However, just like the ages, yuga's and worlds we spoke of earlier, we cycle in and out of this intensely lit belt on a long day night cycle. For each half cycle of 12,000 years, we spend approximately 2,000 of those in the Photon Belt and then back out for another 10,000 years before entering it again for another 2,000 years, completing a 24,000-year cycle.

The last time we cycled through this powerful ring of Light we were on the descending arc of consciousness moving away from the light. This time as we move through this "light belt" we are on the ascending arc of consciousness heading back into the light, so rather than descending into the fear and destruction of the dark ages, it is the time of Ascending/Ascension into Love and Light as we fulfill our highest potential as creators.

Photon energy is divine energy, and photons are messengers of light...they hold knowledge. This intense, high-frequency "radio-active" energy we are being exposed to is vibrating and stimulating our DNA and shifting us on a subatomic level. It is catalyzing rapid change and facilitating the transformation of all life-forms, not just humans, causing the much heralded "shift in consciousness."

Thus, this age, this shift from the Age of Pisces to the

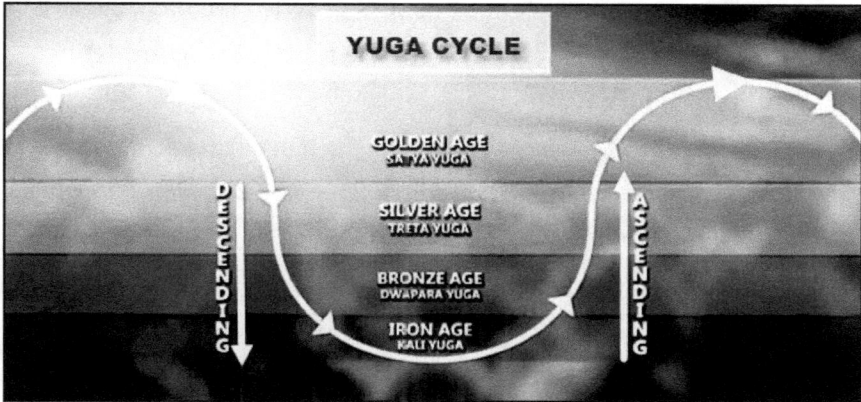

Age of Aquarius is the age of en-LIGHT-enment, the age of great Light, or as the song goes, of "letting the sunshine in." In other words, consciousness "grows up" as we bask in and absorb ever greater and higher frequencies of Light in our 24,000-year descending, ascending cycle of precession, journeying from Light to darkness, and back to Light again.

When our sun (with solar system in tow) has cycled farthest away from its Light sources, consciousness plummets into the dark ages, because of the lack of Light (the Iron/Dark Age, the Kali Yuga). Conversely, when we are basking in great "Light sources" consciousness shifts into high gear.

We are currently receiving and basking in great *Solar Light/Soul-ar Light (Light that feeds our soul)* as we shift positions in the heavens. It is this Light that "quickens" our consciousness/ frequency, causing our DNA shift.

Do you now have a sense of what the consciousness shift is and why it is happening now? Can you see how you are intimately involved, whether you choose to be or not? As humans on this joyride through the heavens, we have completed a cycle of consciousness growth. We have cycled through darkness and back into the Light, thus completing our hero's journey.

The time has come to give "birth" to a new human, a Divine human – an empowered, self-aware, superhuman, a Cosmic Human, the Cosmic Butterfly!

According to famed physicist Nassim Haramein, we are becoming "galactic citizens" as our consciousness shifts from "planetary citizenship to our newly empowered, expansive, galactic citizenship."

Exciting, huh?

Just as a tumbler lock guards her secrets until all the tumblers are properly aligned, so too does the Universe passionately guard her secrets until the time of "alignment." When orbits and cycles align, portals and gateways open, and energy flows unimpeded from the center of the galaxy out to suns, systems, and planets, *bathing all life in higher-frequency light.*

When gateways and portals open, something powerful happens – magic!

A new humanity is unfolding right before our eyes as we dance with these new, photonic, higher-frequency-shifting

DNA codes. These scintillating new frequencies are advancing consciousness and awareness to higher levels of enlightenment/ knowledge, and evolving humans into the next expression of creative force – *superhumans.*

You didn't really think we were at the end, did you? Of course, not. Your heart always whispered ever so gently that there was more...and now this information is in front of you.

NOTES:

Fascinating information has come forth from The Binary Research Institute, explaining that our precession cycle is very likely due to our sun being in a *binary orbit* with/around another star which many, including "Astrotheologist" Santos Bonacci, identify as Sirius.

Walter Cruttenden, Director of the Binary Research Institute and author of *Lost Star of Myth and Time,* explains "Just as the day is one spin of the Earth on its axis, and the year is one revolution of the Earth around the Sun, so too is one Great Year (precession cycle) based on a celestial motion: one orbit of our Sun around its binary center of mass."

In other words, one completed cycle of precession equals one orbit of our sun around its binary partner sun (possibly Sirius), with us in tow.

The Yuga Project film (produced by Cruttenden) states: "Although a new concept to us, some of the earliest astrological records refer to the existence of dual suns. The yogis of ancient India, for example, accepted the binary star-system model as a matter of fact and as the cause of precession."

Furthermore, "Mainstream astronomers are now suggesting that our Sun is part of a binary system. Numerous astronomers including NASA's Davy Kirkpatrick, UCLA's Ned Wright, UC Berkeley's Richard Muller, the University of Louisiana's John Matese and Daniel Whitmire, Caltech's Mike Brown, and others who are observing irregularities in the Oort cloud, the strange orbit of Sedna, and other inexplicable phenomena – are openly suggesting that the Sun is part of a binary system."

And let's not forget that modern science has already determined that most stars dance with a binary partner, so *why not our own sun?*

"Our entire solar system with all its planets and moons describes a huge circle around another sun in space, the star Sirius." *George R. Goodman (early 1900)*

The study of cosmic cycles is fascinating, and even more fun when you begin to "connect the dots" and see with clarity how it all works as a fine-tuned machine. However, it is not the purpose or the intention of this book to prove the precession cycle true or false, nor to investigate its mechanics.

This celebrated cycle *is an accepted fact* that has been recognized in metaphysics, myths, tales, religions, and scientific probes throughout time. It's a very interesting study that you may want to take up for yourself.

Whatever you choose to believe about how or why the precession cycle exists, one thing for sure is that it does exist and, if Plato coined it the "Great Year," then indeed there must be something "great" about it.

My purpose in adding this bit of information about cosmic cycles (the precession cycle) is not so much to educate you on the subject, as it goes way too deep and deserves a book of its own. *Rather, it is included to emphasize what a special time we have entered, one that comes along only once every 24,000 years.*

To summarize:

Cosmic cycles align us with different areas of the heavens and therefore determine how much Light is received and reflected/generated. This in turn dictates our level/density of awareness, the level of consciousness that we have. Light = Consciousness.

When we are not receiving and "basking" in bright Light, we are lacking light, and anytime we are lacking light we are in darkness. Darkness is merely the lack of light – hence, the "Dark Ages," and that includes commensurately limited consciousness and ignorance.

When our sun's position in the heavens is farthest away from the brighter light sources that we intimately dance with consciousness recedes into the Dark Ages, the Kali Yuga; as we move closer to our Light sources, (the sun's binary partner, possibly Sirius, as well as our new position traveling through the Galactic Plane and experiencing the Photon Belt), we are "enlightened" by the Light that carries within it information and wisdom in the form of photons.

The Force

"The sun shines and warms and lights us and we have no curiosity to know why this is so; but we ask the reason of all evil, of pain, and hunger, and mosquitoes and silly people."

– Ralph Waldo Emerson

4

The Cosmic Grid

It's important to recognize that everything is a step-down of energy, from the Central Disc of Light and Love (the Galactic Center) to the Greater Central Suns, and to the Central Suns, which in turn distribute the energy to the suns of solar systems, all the way on down to planets, etc.

Finally, the Light takes up residence in the "suns" of our hearts (the holographic Light/spark/star/sun within us that is essentially us). This pattern plays out throughout the cosmos.

Think of the suns and their cycles as the Galactic Electrical Grid System, the system the galaxy uses to transmit Light and energy/wisdom and knowledge (the creative life force) to all its components.

Just as our own electrical grid system has step-downs and transfer stations, so too does the galaxy have its own system of "electromagnetic transfer stations" via suns, planets, moons, comets, etc. They all play a role. No-thing is just "hanging" out in the sky.

As above, so below is a universal truth. Who do you think we are copying, and where do you believe we get ideas for our own earthly systems? From the heavens, of course! They are written into our energetic frequency.

The patterns are there; we just tune into them. It is the physics and operation of the Universe of Love and Light, and we cannot detach our own little world from this. We are an integral part of all of it.

Ours is a very structured and orderly Universe, *with all of us working together toward the same purpose.* Everything, including every orb in the cosmos, is alive and connected with a definite purpose in line with Divine Will. That's why we're referred to as systems and universes – because we operate within a system of Unity, not independently.

Those celestial "twinkling crystal gems" are not just hanging out in the heavens, sparkling and looking pretty for pretty's sake. They are critical players, receiving and transmitting energy and light, bathing all life forms in higher-frequency light.

Without that light, there can be no life.

It's exciting to realize how powerful, cosmic energy portals are lining up, causing major energy alignments and adjustments that are resulting in this huge evolutionary leap in consciousness.

Cosmic energy is interacting with Earth's energy matrix, causing changes within matter and Light. *This in turn increases the vibrational frequencies of all physical forms of matter. That includes you and me.*

Earth is not the only planet evolving (if it revolves, it evolves). The whole Cosmos is stepping up to another level and expression of Love. Everything is evolving, and the light frequencies produced and arriving from deep within the cosmos (the energy, the Love) are affecting our electromagnetic beings as heat does to ice or water, and the result is a *"quickening,"* an expansion of consciousness. Just as ice transforms to steam given the proper amount of heat, our atoms and molecules, warmed by Love, are really dancing.

It is the energy of Love that heats our consciousness/ hearts. Put another way, *it is "Love that melts a cold, cold heart."*

Ruby Nelson in The Door of Everything states: *"The vibratory rate of each individual cell will be gradually quickened, or speeded up, by the power contained in these rays of spiritual Light."*

A very important point to understand and remember is that everything you think, feel, say, and do passes through your energetic matrix first; it comes through/*vibrates through your atoms.* Your electromagnetic system is exposed to these vibrations as they travel out from you. You are the first exposed and you receive the intensity of what you give out.

If it is the frequency of Love, then you are the first to receive its healing energy. If it is fear/judgment, anger, or guilt, you too are the first to be impacted by these energies.

We are currently shifting from rigidity to fluidity in our conscious understanding and expression of Love. It is a new cycle, and along with it are new perceptions, new understandings, and clarity of Love, the Unity – the energy of Life. That's what the fuss about December 2012 (and, these times in general) is about, and rightly so. I stress this to awaken you to the fact that these are *special times* we are in. *You need to understand that.*

We're on the cusp of the Aquarian Age…the Age of Light and Love…the age when the *"sun shines in" and lights up our consciousness.*

....

"All our life patterns are pre-synchronized to the motion of the celestial bodies. We can ignore their existence, but we cannot avoid encountering their effects."

— *Swami Nityananda Saraswati*

....

The Conscious Leap

"It is the stars, the stars above us,
that govern our conditions."

– William Shakespeare

5

Ascension

T his new "light energy," that is affecting all of us, is literally expanding and evolving human consciousness into beings who know. We are becoming self-aware and this process is appropriately called ascension. It is *ascension in consciousness,* an expansion and raising of our energetic frequency, and all of us are participating. No one is exempt.

It is, without a doubt, the most exciting time there has ever been to be alive and conscious as a human. *For the first time ever, we are making this huge leap in evolution with conscious intent, shifting from one dimension into another while we are alive, incarnate and aware of what is happening.*

There is a reason for that. This is the first time in any dimension we've experienced so far that we are empowered to be self-aware. So, it follows that when we make this leap, it must be a conscious leap, a conscious decision, a self-aware decision, an empowered decision – *an intended decision*.

What does that mean? It means that death is being eliminated for those who choose life. Hopefully, that struck a chord within you! Remember, the caterpillar did not die but transformed right here on Earth from one expression to another. The Bible (*I Cor.15:26*) clearly states that "The last enemy that shall be destroyed is death."

This high-powered, Light-filled, electromagnetic, photonic energy (remember, we are talking vibration of forces) affecting us from different Light sources, awakens within us dormant patterns of DNA as it *fills our cells with Light*. It literally shines away the shadows/darkness (the lower-frequency thoughts/patterns/programs) – the ones that have held us captive to our survival/ dual-minded programming and opens us to a much greater expression of the Divine. The photon belt, suns, solar flares, Supernova 1987a, and Eta Carinae (my favorite star system/supernova) are all active participants. They (among others) are receivers and generators of Light, bequeathing this new, empowered DNA.

DNA, often called the "language of light," is affected and changed when it bathes in galactically generated light, and our new position and alignment in the heavens allows this. As planet Earth's energies begin to intensify, the human body, which is electromagnetic in nature, also evolves and intensifies. We are transforming as a species. How exciting is that?

Annalee Skarin, author of many books on Immortality of the physical body including "The Temple of God" states,

"An atom is Spirit in essence. A ray of radiant force curled upon itself. It is but a ray of the very Spirit of God." A very important piece of information when you realize that your body is simply an assortment of atoms.

Light is a carrier of information via photons; this is not wishful thinking but *scientific fact*. (Think crystals, and how they hold information via light.) It is said that the mystical crystal skulls displayed in museums and private collections (Indiana Jones and the Kingdom of the Crystal Skull comes to mind) can hold more information than any of today's largest supercomputers.

Cell-phone companies are doing extensive research on the pineal gland, a gland located in the center of the brain which has miniscule crystals all over it. They are looking at the pineal gland as the cell phone of the future because of the information it can receive and generate via its crystals.

As this high-powered light/photonic energy affects our electromagnetic being (our consciousness), *our knowledge, understanding, and participation in and as Love is expanding.* Entering through the chakras (vortexes of energy...our main energy centers), this energy is distributed throughout our glands/endocrine system and electrical system, finding its way to the center of every atom that forms our bodies.

In other words, our electromagnetic cellular structure is being tuned to absorb more light energy. You'll recall that light is a carrier of information/knowledge, so the greater light/energy we hold/release, the deeper is our understanding, knowledge, clarity, and expression of Love.

Sounds complicated, but it isn't. Just think energy, vibration, frequency, etc. We are energetic beings affected by our new position in the heavens and this newly arriving higher-frequency energy. It is shifting our conscious awareness (our frequency), awakening encodings in our "dormant" DNA and expanding our expression/consciousness of Love. We literally *become* this new expansive Light as our frequency rises to resonate with it.

You cannot see this energy any more than you can "see" electricity...but you are feeling it, as everyone is. Who can deny that there are major changes happening all over the Earth, including climate changes, which are directly tied to consciousness? Things are turbulent, things are shifting; *things are changing*.

Nick Anthony Fiorenza summed these times up quite nicely…

"Earth begins to retune/return to galactic awareness and the inpouring light begins to avalanche—and all of life on Earth begins its transmutation and illumination—from the inside-out."

The Universal Song of Love

"If it might be so expressed, the energy of thought, or mind force, in its totality, reaches the solar system from a distant cosmic centre via Sirius. Sirius acts the transmitter, or the focalising centre, whence emanate those influences which produce self-consciousness in man."

– Alice Bailey

6

A Serious/Sirius Tune-up

The Uni-verse is the verse/song of Unity that lives in every heart. *It is the Universal song of Love, the Unity-Verse.*

As one's consciousness/frequency ascends and expands to absorb greater Light, lingering frequencies of a lower vibration, surface to be transmuted. The same principle applies to Mother Earth as she ascends and evolves. She is working through and ridding herself of all lower vibrations that are attached to her (our distorted creations). These manifest as storms, floods, fires, and other so-called "acts of God."

This is Mother Nature's way of cleansing and readying herself for her own ascension, her new vibration, her new frequency/ heartbeat. She is a living BEING. *If she were not herself alive, she could not produce life.* The Schumann Resonance, considered to be the heartbeat of Mother Earth, is increasing in speed. This supports people's subjective impressions of time speeding up.

Since you are an integral part of nature, on a personal level, you will be presented with "opportunities" that seem to come in the difficult guise of "storms." This is simply your own consciousness ridding itself of distorted energy/perceptions that need transmuting via higher frequencies. They are being brought to your *conscious attention* for transmuting and tuning.

In other words, we are all getting a *serious* tune-up – or quite possibly, a "Sirius tune-up" to be in harmony with the Universe, the Uni-Verse or Unity-Verse of Love, whether we know it or not.

Those who play musical instruments realize how important it is that their instruments stay in tune if they are to create harmonious music. As instruments in the Galactic Orchestra, we are being "fine-tuned" so that we may go forth and create beautiful, harmonious, bliss-filled music in harmony with the Symphony of Love, the Universe...the Unity-Verse.

Just as a drop of water holds the fullness of the water from which it sprang, as sparks of the Infinite, we are the fullness of Source energy, the energy we spring from. Source frequency is Love, and therefore our authentic frequency is Love. *We are the frequency of Love – literally!*

If you expect to create beautiful, harmonious music (the song of your life), then you must be in tune, aligned with your one true frequency, *your one true authentic vibration,*

"Love." The vibrating "note" of your every thought, feeling, word, or deed that is out of alignment with Love must be tuned until it vibrates fully and harmoniously in the frequency of Love. Are you in tune? Are you producing beautiful sweet music or are you producing distorted disharmony in your music, in your life?

The information shared here teaches you *how to align, tune in to, play and harmonize* with this newly arriving expansive frequency of Love, this new high-powered energy arriving from the cosmos. You will move out of linear time and ascend from lower densities of consciousness – separation, duality, cause-and-effect, past and future, and rigidity of thought – to the fluid dimension of Unity and Love.

You'll move beyond any resistance within you as this new energy activates in your subconscious everything that needs clearing (is of a slower frequency), to resonating and creating with this power. Your new playground will be the 5th dimension, *the realm of the "present."*

This is about consciously participating with creation; it's about aligning with your passion, your purpose and power, and playing with magic. You were created to be conscious creators – that is your purpose and why you have a consciousness with the ability to know yourself.

It is the action and expression of Love, the passion-in-motion that shifts energy, that transmutes energy, that moves energy, that CREATES!

Consciously creating is participating with creation as it happens now, in the moment. It is spontaneous, exciting, fun, playful, surprising, and magical. It is about transmuting and playing consciously with energy in alignment with Divine Will, Divine Mind, now where life/action happens.

We have reached the point in creation where Source is empowered to Love itself consciously. It is a beautiful and empowering reality!

....

We are connecting to the Alchemist, the Magician, and the Wizard within.

....

The 5th Dimension

*We are celebrating a cosmic
birthday and our gift to the
Universe is our "presence"
...our awareness of the magic
of the "present."*

7

The Magic Moment

OK, so now we understand enough about densities, dimensions, and consciousness to know we want to be 5th-dimensional in nature because *that's where all the magic and fun is.* How do we get there? What's the roadmap to this dimension? Is there a shortcut?

We've already established that linear time exists in the lower dimensions where our dual mind honors fear, scrambles for survival, and plays with the concept of duality – of past and future, good and bad, and cause and effect.

The Ancient Mayans were keen star watchers and Master Calendar Keepers who studied cosmic cycles. Their Long Count Calendar is a precise mathematical system with an end date given as 2012. They knew it was the end of one grand cosmic cycle and the beginning of another cycle.

"According to their ancient prophecy, in 2012 the old-World Age of Delusion and Deception would draw to a close, as the human

race transforms from its ego-driven fixation on materialism and limited belief systems to its connection with the eternal Higher-Self."

In other words, these advanced stargazers, never predicted catastrophe in 2012. Their calendars revealed that it "would be the end of time as we know it," and that humanity was to shift to the "fifth sun" phase, wherein lay a "Golden Age" of higher consciousness.

If we are consciously moving out of past and future into the present moment (in thought), then we are moving out of linear time into the fluidity of "*now.*" If we have no past and future in thought, then we have no time (as we currently know it) right in line with the Mayan prediction ofgg "the end of time as we know it."

What we do have left is the present moment, the power of Now. Now is the *gift*, the *present* we receive when we consciously play in the 5th dimension, where discovery, excitement, and exploration take place without judgments, condemnations, and personal opinions.

Now is the realm of knowledge. It's where excitement is felt, as our outer senses join with our inner senses in a melody of miraculous play!

Work came into existence when we fell in consciousness... *when our inner senses (feminine, intuitive side) shut down and our outer senses (male, logical side) took over –* at which point we consciously woke up in the world of physical form. Survival, fear, and protection was the order of the day. Everything outside of us became suspect because we no longer felt our *inner connection* to Source, to Love, to all things. We no longer saw Oneness/Unity, and thus fear (in the form of protection) took over and has been our ruling master ever since.

Let's face it: It's hard to meditate when you're beating off an animal who is trying to eat you for dinner. *Survival demanded attention.* Our full focus was thrown into the outer world and dictated by our physical senses for good reason.

However, do we really have to continue to "work hard" to consciously manifest/create something in our lives? Are we destined to be stuck at this level of understanding and creating for eternity? Are we still playing the game of survival, of "good guys and bad guys?" If we are shifting into higher dimensions of awareness, shouldn't these dimensions have different rules? Shouldn't creation become easier as we gain and hold greater Light, more Love?

Absolutely, without a doubt, it should.

What would be the purpose of evolution if the game didn't change, get easier, more exciting, enlightening and fun? Without those enticements, we would soon lose the will to reach beyond what we presently are. What would be the purpose? There must be a purpose.

And, speaking of doubt, this may be a good time to address those doubts of yours. You must leave all your doubts behind. The lower vibration of doubt (doubt is resistance) has no place in the higher frequencies of Love; neither does effort. What does effort have to do with playing? Playing is flowing in the excitement and discovery of life with ease. The only effort involved is your focus on consciously aligning with the moment and expressing Love regardless of what your logic wants to convince you of.

Remember, this is all about connecting with the energy of Love, and Love is magical and spontaneous and requires no effort. It is not effort we should be exerting, but alignment with this power. We must resonate with this eternal "frequency flow."

When you remove your attention (your conscious alignment) from the present moment for any reason and place it on one of the many dramas/traumas/trivialities in life that are continually vying for your attention, you have *descended in consciousness.* You are operating from lower, denser frequencies – survival, victim, and duality consciousness.

After all, who's enjoying this conscious moment if you're off in your head playing a role in that drama of yours?

Obviously, it's not a crime, and there is no judgment involved for you are always exactly where you need to be; however, you have lost your greatest gift, the present. As each snowflake contributes to the art of creation in its own unique way, so too is each moment sacred and new, original and unique, never to be seen or experienced in the same way again.

The moment is magical if we are present.

....

The Time of Global Change Is at Hand

*What is the end of the world for some is a
New World for those who realize it is.*

*To surrender logistical mind to galactic
awareness is to surrender fear to Love.*

*What was, shall no longer be.
What was not, can now become.*

– Nick Anthony Fiorenza

....

The Force

*"If you pray quickly to me for help,
without much feeling except
perhaps that of desperation, then
return to the former mental
attitudes of fear and doubting,
putting your strength behind these
attitudes, which becomes your
prayer? Which drops into the great
subconscious reservoir, the quick
plea for help or the predominant,
steady attitudes to which your
feelings cling?"*

— Ruby Nelson

8

The Power of Now

What good is it to imagine yourself happy and healthy, with abundance flowing into the future of your life, in your daydreams, if what you are *consciously* feeling, entertaining, and experiencing *now* are sad, depressed, fearful thoughts?

Which one of these two realities is real? Of course, what you are in the moment is real, nothing else. Everything else is a figment of your imagination.

Although imagination is the greatest creative tool there is because it allows us to bypass our restrictive thinking minds, *if you don't bring the emotion of what you are imagining into the present moment, everything you have "imagined in" remains in your daydreams.*

There is nothing wrong with imagining. *The problem begins when we leave our imaginings in our imagination and consciously go back to our mind issues.*

If you *perceive yourself* (and act accordingly) as happy, healthy, and abundant NOW, then that is what you are! If you perceive yourself as sad, depressed, and fearful (and act accordingly), then that is what you are! Your life expresses NOW...not in some imaginary future or deceased past!

Imagining is powerful, but it is not the completion of creation, it is the beginning. You must take what you've "imaged-in" and live it through your actions NOW, where creation happens.

In other words, you cannot experience happiness in your life until you bring the emotion into the present moment. You can imagine yourself as happy, but until you live that emotion NOW...until you experience it NOW where creation happens, it is but a daydream that vanishes the second your attention is withdrawn.

Think about that. Your world is a manifestation of what you are now (exactly what your perceptions/resonance/vibrations are in the moment), not what you are wishing to be! And since you can only BE in the MOMENT, then *it is what you ARE in the moment that expresses your life*; not what you are imagining in your future. What you are imagining in the future remains in the future. You must BE what you desire your life to be NOW to experience it now. Otherwise it remains in the realm of your imagination. It remains in the future of your mind.

Sure, you created it, and yes, it is real and lives within your imagination and you can revisit it anytime you want – in your imagination. But you can never experience it physically until you bring it into the world you want to experience it in, the physical world of form.

That's the fullness and completion of creation. Your imagination enables you to dream of being anything you want; it bypasses your restrictive mind and connects you with "all possibility." After "seeing" your visions on your inner screen, you must finish the process of creation (you are only halfway done). You have not yet taken that energy from the realm of imaginings into the realm of physical manifestation, and the only way to do that is to energetically BE IT where creation happens…in the MOMENT.

The past and future are about thinking, labeling and defining. Now is about living the experience. If you truly believe it…then you will BE it. You will act the part. And, that's the completion of creation.

If you create an ideal life for yourself in your imagination but you then express "fear" about your coming bills in the moment where creation happens, which of the two do you believe is going to manifest? What you are in the moment (consciously) is always what manifests. How could it be otherwise? It is what your energetic signature is expressing.

What you want to experience must be felt now, the only reality! If you want to experience happiness, then you must *"be happy" now. You simply cannot experience what you are not energetically expressing!*

You cannot bring creation to you. You cannot make happiness rely on persons, places, or things. You are the creator, and all comes from within, where the controls are.

Joy, happiness, contentment, bliss...they are not found without in external circumstances. These divine virtues are all elements of your true authentic self. You do not have to create happiness – you are happiness! *But you must consciously claim it, and the only way to consciously claim it is to "be it," and the only place you can "be it" is the moment where action takes place and creation happens.*

If you want abundance, then you must express abundance in your energy signature. If your energy signature is dark with financial fears, how can you expect to experience abundance? If your energy signature is filled with fear, anger and hate, how can you expect to experience Love and all the joys of Love?

Remember, this is all about frequency. You must match the frequency of what it is you want to experience *now.*

If you want abundance, then be abundant in your thoughts, words, and actions. Give abundance to others in whatever form you can give, and you shall be the first to experience the "feeling" as it goes out from you and abundance shall be yours.

Don't you see? As you give abundance to others this "feeling" permeates your cells first. It is what you are in the moment, and the moment is the only reality.

If you want peace, give this feeling to others by being it. You shall then be the first to experience the vibration and peace will then be yours. If it is happiness and joy you are after, then offer these things generously, and you shall be in the moment all these things yourself.

What does it matter what you are dreaming about your future when the only reality lives in the present moment? *Life happens now…the only place action can take place.* You must BE what you want to see, and there is simply no way around this. Just as the Law of Attraction is a powerful creative law, so too is the Law of Resonance for it responds to whatever you are in the moment.

Your future never comes, when it does appear it is now. Now is the only real existence there is; *life is a series of now moments that you are creating moment to moment.*

Here's the key:

The only place you can express, and experience life is the moment where you can act and engage your physical senses, where you can actually BE what you want to see in your world.

Your past consists of memories, your future of imaginings, but reality lives now, in the moment. It is about your actions, beliefs/perceptions, expressions, and feelings right now. That's all that matters.

You can dream it, imagine it, and want it forever, but until you live it now (fill it with ~*live*~ *energy by being it*) you will never experience it in the physical realm, the realm of form.

The world you see about you is a result of creation, just as everyone's world is. Everything you see – the whole world – is a result of creation. The problem has been that we did not recognize the creator as ourselves! It did not occur to us that we alone have the power to create and change our lives and the world about us because we alone created our lives.

When we don't recognize ourselves as the creator, we don't realize the power we wield as creators to change things. By taking responsibility for the moment and all it contains, you recognize the power that you are that created this situation, and it's this recognition and acceptance that empowers you to change it.

If you can accept that you had the power to create it, then you are empowered to change it.

When you eliminate all fears, titles, judgments, condemnations, borders, barriers, limits and personal opinions that live in your mind, what are you left with? Love, the undivided, whole, potential of ALL THINGS; the essence of eternity and power of "now."

You must remove yourself from the "blame game." Every experience in your life has been a service by Love to bring you closer to Love.

All fears, titles, judgments, condemnations and personal opinions live in the past and future of your mind. Clean up your mind, get rid of your personal story/drama, and all that is left is Love.

The Creative Principle

"Ideas are simply a chemical electromagnetic event. Ideas have no form until such time as they are brought into action and form."

– Albert Einstein

9

Attraction Action

The Law of Attraction *is a powerful creative law,* but you are not going to manifest anything just sitting there daydreaming. I can assure you of that. The one word that is obvious, but generally unrecognized within attraction is the power behind the Law of Attraction. And that word, that power, is ACTION!

The simple but essential element powering the Law of Attraction is action. "To attract we must act." And, the only realm we can act in is the present moment, right now.

Action is the prelude to form, the KEY to manifesting/creating in the physical realm, and it can only take place in the present moment.

Has the light gone off in your head yet?

Where does your consciousness need to dwell if you want to be *consciously creating*? In the present moment, in the now. Focus your attention, your awareness, your consciousness in the here and now, where spontaneous action/manifestation and magical creation take place.

It's a beautiful exchange of ~~energy~~

The Universe gifts you with the "present," you in return gift the Universe with your "presence." An incredibly powerful alignment!

You acknowledge the gift of the present when you put your attention, your presence, your awareness/energy/focus on the gift of the present. You are then participating with creation because you are consciously attuned to it, resonating with it, aligned with it and ONE with IT!

There's magic in that paragraph.

You simply don't need to look any further than the present moment. When you align yourself this way, intuition becomes your guide and synchronicity your playground. Every step is brought to your conscious attention in the present moment, each one opening the door to the next.

Your only job is to pay attention in the moment and take the appropriate *action* as it reveals itself *in the moment.*

Synchronous events begin to happen on a consistent basis. But you must be paying attention; you must act when the opportunity presents itself in the now. You must be synchronized with the opportunity and you do this by keeping your energy, your awareness, your conscious attention and focus aligned *in the moment* where *Love and all potential live and express.*

You let go of the past and future of your mind, of the good and bad and cause and effect of whatever draws you away from the moment, and you enter a new world of creating from all possibility by acting *now in the moment.*

Intuition never speaks through your thoughts – when you're lost in your subconscious programming, creating some sort of drama about your past or future, some sort of drama in your mind. *It is a present-moment experience* and one you want to get very familiar with because...

That's where the magic is.

"The music is always created in the moment." Merlin

This new energy is about *playing in the present,* consciously creating and returning to magic, wholeness, and Oneness with Source as fully conscious Divine creative beings.

Just think – the Cosmos has evolved self-aware containers through which to manifest Divine Will. In other words, these minds of ours become *servants in service to Love/Divine Will,* which expresses through the heart and is always the pathway to our most perfect expression.

Action is what moves and shifts energy in form. We are the "action takers," the ones who bring the creative process from the "image screen, the imagination" into physical form. From image to creation, from inspiration to form, it takes the full man, one whose heart and mind are functioning as a synchronized and complementary team, to *consciously create.*

The heart is empowered to give the signal, the inspiration, the love, and the mind is empowered to carry it out in form by acting in the moment *where creation happens.*

Without action, a vision remains a vision and never comes to fruition.

The Secret

"I don't teach my people to pray because their prayers will harm them. Right now, they are not conscious enough to ask for anything, and whatsoever they ask will be wrong. First, let them become conscious enough. I teach them how to become more conscious and then it is up to them."

– Gautama Buddha

10

"Let There Be Light"

T he *Law of Attraction* has been misrepresented and bandied about so much these days that most people no longer understand its power or primacy, nor do they believe they are empowered to consciously operate and use this law to change their lives.

Because it has not been understood with full clarity, there has been more disappointment experienced with attempted use of the LOA than success. The reputation of this powerful law has been temporarily tarnished as misguided people (those operating in lower frequencies of consciousness) choose to blame the law for their seeming "failures" rather than searching to understand why the law is not working as they believe it should.

However, damaged reputation or not, this immutable law is always in effect and is still operating perfectly today as it has since, well, forever! You cannot remove a law from the very foundations that it built. To remove the law would be to destroy the structure. This law is always in perfect operation.

The key, the secret to how this law operates, is this:

The LOA is an immutable law that works in *all dimensions.* It is how creation happens. The key is knowing that *it must operate/play by the rules of whatever dimension it is operating in.* (Remember, each dimension has its own rules.)

When acting within the constraints of lower dimensions/ densities of consciousness, LOA is subject to/must operate under duality/polarity rules – under "cause and effect" and past and future – all our definitions and labels for things. It operates under split powers, with the "head/logic" separate from the "heart/feeling" nature. *The heart wants to "feel" its way through with excitement and discovery, but the mind wants to inject "logic" and protection.*

Therefore, when you attempt to activate the LOA while operating in a lower state of consciousness, you create through *divided thinking* because that's where your perception/belief system is operating from, division. Mirroring this uncertainty, results are generally mixed, maddeningly delayed, short-lived or not at all.

Your belief in "past and future" and "cause and effect," your perceptions attached to lower-density concepts of duality and separation, are operating this great law from those limited duality concepts.

You are the operator, so how could you possibly create anything other than that which is within the confines of your own conscious rules? If you want to change how you create, you must shift the realm you create from, your consciousness.

Rather than create from the slower realm of limiting laws, karma, and time (the realm the mind operates from), why not take the "high road," where you *create consciously* in the moment? Why not play in the realm of eternity, the easier, more glorious and fun way to create from Unity, rather than within the realm of time, where karma is created through the belief in cause and effect?

In this realm of *Now/Eternity*, your frequency (consciousness) is in alignment and operating within the frequency of 5D Unity – Love consciousness. No personal opinions, limits, or labels are blocking your view of "all possibilities" and slowing down your frequency here.

Fifth-dimensional consciousness playfully creates in the present where "all possibility but awaits the command for creation, *for nothing can be created without the creative command.*

And, what is this great creative command? It is: *"Let there be Light."* And what is this Light? It is your conscious focused awareness/attention/energy/intention in the moment where creation/*action* happens.

Whenever you focus your attention/energy on something, you are "shedding light" on it and completing the greatest creative command ever given, "Let there be Light."

Conscious creation demands that awareness remain in the present moment where "the passions of the heart meet and dance with inspired action, and creation happens." Both your heart and your mind must be joined in sacred "matrimony," operating as one unit, a unified force with One purpose, before you can realize the gift of conscious creation. Until then, you will continue to create from the lower, slower dimensions of time/cause and effect.

"The heart is a magnet for source energy, and when the heart and mind are unified in purpose, creation is direct and unfiltered, whereas in a separated heart/mind, creation is indirect and filtered through the veil of separation, subject to cause and effect." Lauren Carolyn Gorgo

The heart operates in the moment. It is a unified field of consciousness and knows nothing of past or future. Those are all constructs/dramas of the mind. You must get your mind out of your past and future and into the moment where it is aligned with the power of the heart/Love and spontaneous unprogrammed action.

Because 5D consciousness is anchored in the "now," our intentions sent from the heart are not polarized and creation is not subject to personal, old, subconscious programming or limiting concepts. They don't resonate here. They are expressions of lower levels of consciousness and must be shed before entrance to the 5th dimension of expanded Love is possible.

The present is the playground of 5D consciousness wherein you are the fullness of creation itself and lack nothing. Without personal restrictions everything becomes yours to choose and experience without limits! This "mix and match" of possibilities awaits you! It is the playground of eternity, the playground of all potential and all possibility, open to your unlimited and empowered imagination!

Much like a snake sheds its old skin for a new one, we are shedding our old, worn-out consciousness – with its limits, labels, and oppressive constraints – for freedom.

When you operate from the 5th dimension, you are aligned with and vibrating with your pure authentic frequency of Love, which wants nothing more than to grant your every heartfelt desire, dream, and wish – right now.

But here's the secret to this whole process:

Because you are the creator, the energy for these creations must come from you – from your conscious attention, command, and focus ("Let there be Light") of energy in the moment where conscious creation takes place.

According to quantum physicist Pascual Jordan, in the field of quantum theory: *"Observations not only disturb what is to be measured, they produce it."*

You hold the key to creation. You are either creating *consciously* from the 5th dimension, the "present moment" or *subconsciously* from your past and future. *Wherever your attention is, whatever your focus is on, your creation is also, because you are the creator.*

Do you see how this process works?

When operating as creator from the 5th dimension of awareness (Unified Love Consciousness), you are empowered to command Light *consciously* because you are operating consciously, putting you in full control.

If you are *consciously* out of the moment and into the past or future of your mind, you are creating from past experiences or future expectations – *both of which have no validity in the moment.* You might compare it to running old programming on your computer and expecting new results (attention on the past) or, expecting results from a program you have yet to see (attention on the future)!

Results happen now, where action takes place. It is the eternal moment – moment to moment, where Love, magic, and intuition abide. When consciously connected to the moment, you are aligned with eternity, where all possibility exists to express Joy. You are *consciously connected* to Love, where all your dreams and wishes are eternal realities that you recognize and embrace in the Light of your conscious command/attention/intention.

The Law of Attraction as it operates within lower dimensions is about manifesting in your future after you work and toil (pay your dues) to bring desired outcomes. (Those are the rules of the lower dimensions, where limited thoughts and perceptions rule.) Where "if this, then that" mentality, the "past and future" scenario are in operation.

As we've seen, the problem with trying to create this way is that your mind is constantly in your subconscious thoughts, trying to create something in your future or change something from your past. But, if your awareness is in the past or future, how do you expect to manifest *now*, where creation happens?

Your awareness/focus is the creative force. It is the Light of creation. When you are consciously focused in the moment you are in the flow and creating from all possibility. This flow is free but can only be accessed in the present moment because *the moment is where this energy flows.*

When you focus on the past or future (working from your subconscious mind), your creation is subject to whatever labels and limitations live there. On the other hand, when your conscious attention/awareness is in the present moment, you have the power to consciously create by your command. And, what is this command?

"Let there be Light." Your focused attention is the light...(the observer in Quantum Physics).

Quantum physicist Danah Zohar analyzed quantum-like behavior and concludes that consciousness functions according to the laws of quantum mechanics. In other words, consciousness expresses through the world of quantum mechanics. Whatever you place your attention on changes from a wave into a particle. *You are a powerful creator.*

Consciousness that is specific to lower dimensions has many conflicts between what the subconscious and conscious minds are wanting. The subconscious, operating from fear and in survival mode, defensively battles and denies what the perfect blueprint of the heart is revealing. Because it operates from "protection mode," it is ever on the lookout for problems to deal with. This "battle" can slow creation of desired outcomes to a crawl (caterpillar flashbacks).

Operating the Law of Attraction within 5th dimensional consciousness, is about creating now as you align your energy/awareness/attention (creative command "Let there be Light") with inspired action in the moment. This enables perfection to move through you without resistance, personal opinions, opposition, or force!

As the action-takers, we have the privilege of expressing and completing the creative process here on Earth. We bring Divine inspiration into physical manifestation so that the creative process is complete and reaches its fullest potential.

According to the Law of One… "Light is intelligent, full of energy and the building block of what we call matter." 13.9

In Summary:

The Law of Creation, or what is commonly known as the Law of Attraction, works perfectly in whatever dimension you are consciously aligned with or resonate with. It is law and indifferent to circumstances. What does change, however, and what does matter when using these powerful creative laws is your point of perception.

As the operator, you must choose the dimension/perception from which you will consciously use the LOA. The lower, slower dimensions of "work and toil" (the realm of repetition and protection) or the 5th dimension of now/Eternity, of play and magic, where excitement and "all possibility" awaits your command. It is the ever-present moment, *where the voice of intuition is easily heard* and conveys true action. The choice is always yours.

The joy, the ease, the empowerment, and the magic of operating the LOA are realized the moment you *consciously* align with 5D Unity/Love consciousness and create from all possibility rather than the tiny box of limited perceptions and conditions programmed in your subconscious mind.

The Perpetual Playground

The intuitive mind is a sacred gift, and the rational mind is a faithful servant. We have created a society that honors the servant and has forgotten the gift.

11

Playing in the Present

Thus far we've established that creation/manifestation happens in the present where action takes place, and that we must align ourselves with the present if we want to be conscious creators. *Simple, huh?*

Currently we are exercising our subconscious minds and creating that which is no longer, or that which we hope – or fear – is yet to be. Creating in the present asks us to create from the heart, from inspired feelings/images – *to create without input from the programmed, subconscious mind.*

We must leave the opinions of our mind at the door and create using the feelings we receive from our heart. Not the chaotic untrained emotions, but the *inspired intuitive feelings*.

Whoa! Even as I write these words, I can feel resistance from the minds reading that sentence!

Goodness gracious! How in the world do I go about operating in life without using my mind?

We've already established that conscious creation manifests spontaneously in the present, whereas the subconscious mind operates from the past and future. When you allow the subconscious to rule your life and create your experiences – rather than embracing the crystalline consciousness of what you are presently experiencing – you are likely bringing the same scenario back onto yourself over and over and your life is pretty much a repetition of experiences.

This explains why you may feel like a hamster on a wheel, going around and round only to end up in the same spot.

Why? Because the past is the entirety of what the subconscious knows, it can only draw and create from within the limits of what it has experienced in the past – the stored memories (pleasant and not so pleasant), programs, comedies, tragedies, and traumas, all neatly organized and filed away for future reference. It's a heck of a filing system!

For the most part, this is what you've been using to create your world. You are continually projecting the past (by tapping into your subconscious for probabilities and answers) onto the blank screen of your future. It appears in your now because that is what you are currently projecting. Your life always reflects what you are now.

By dwelling in past experiences, you recreate them because that is what your attention, your energy, your intended command of Light is on and creation happens.

In other words, "when you look to the past to create your future, your future will mirror your past."

But the wonderful news is that we are going through a huge system upgrade. No longer must you limit yourself to lower densities/dimensions of thinking and slogging through solutions and decisions based on dead, worn-out experiences. You can tap into all possibility as a 5th dimensional non-thinker who plays with creation as it happens now!

You do not think about the moment. You experience the moment, you live the moment, whereas you think about the past or future. Thinking takes you away from the gift of the moment, the "present" that the Universe has given you.

Although the subconscious serves an honorable purpose, protecting us as we're navigating through survival mode, we must eventually take the rudder and steer our own ship. Otherwise, it has no choice but to continue "protecting" us at all costs – even at the cost of cheating us out of real-time experiences. We can liken it to radiation therapy. Sure, the radiation kills the cancer cells, but it also wipes out many of the good ones.

The subconscious itself is not the problem. *What's currently stored there is.* Everything presently stored has been formulated *from a mind that thinks it is separate,* and therefore can think only in protective, dualistic terms. It's all about the opposing forces of good and bad, and cause and effect. Resulting behavior stems from the emotion of fear – fear based on threats to physical survival, and even threats to the nonphysical ego! It is these tyrannical perceptions and assumptions – the files, the beliefs, patterns, programs, and systems, that need to be dealt with.

That's what the personal mind, often referred to as "ego," uses to build your world. It creates dramas to star in because that is what gives and sustains its life. Without those dramas, it has no life.

But things are shifting…

On the horizon a new world awaits us along with a new and easy way of creating, an advanced way for those who resonate with this Light vibration and energy of Love. If you think connecting to an electric power source can be explosive, wait until you connect to the force of Unity, the *original Source of power – Love*. What a charge it's been so far! From Homo erectus to Homo sapiens to Homo luminous – and I can only imagine what might come after that!

Your current physical body is morphing as your consciousness rises in understanding, clarity, acceptance, and expression of intended Love. When your aura is pure and free of all discordant vibrations, it is aligned with Love, and every cell in your body explodes with Light. You are then the proud owner of a 5th-dimensional Light Body, the vehicle that you will use to transition into higher realms of Love as you continue your *conscious journey* into Eternity. You have aligned with your Light Body Merkaba (Merkabah). "Mer" means Light, "Ka" means Spirit, and "Ba" means Body. "Merkabah" is the Hebrew word for chariot.

Counter-rotating fields of light often referred to as "wheels within wheels," or "spirals of energy/DNA" surround the Merkabah and are used to transport your spirit/Light-body from one dimension to another through frequency. It is your chariot of transportation through higher dimensions and the energy vehicle you will use to connect and communicate with those in higher realms, just as Ascended Masters do.

You didn't really think this was the end, did you? Why in the world would life have evolved this far only to stop? How could it be that life evolved through the mineral, plant, animal, and human kingdoms only to run out of inspiration?

If that were the plan, we would be leaving an increasingly abused Mother Earth with all her children's ignorance and woes as we gleefully ascended to some Heaven beyond Earth. Hardly seems fair, considering that Mother Earth gave us life, nurtured and sustained us in every way. Every drop of water that hydrates us, every morsel of food that nourishes us, every shelter that protects us has been given to us by Mother Earth.

Cutting out on her would mean that Mother Earth had no purpose other than to serve as a battleground for our dramas until we decided to move to more pleasant realms, leaving our Mother to die in the wake of our garbage. *I can't think of anything more selfish.* Is this how we would treat our own mother? Should we be preparing ourselves to make it to some sort of imagined heaven in some sort of imagined future while Mother Earth is left to suffer the life-threatening imbalances we leave behind?

That is separate thinking at its worst! We divide ourselves off from Mother Earth as though we have no connection and that is the single cause of all our ills. We do not acknowledge our connection to everyone and everything, starting with nature, with Mother Earth – and with the Cosmos.

The Universe has a much grander plan in place for Mother Earth than for her to just serve as our stomping ground. Yes, she has served us loyally and, in every way imaginable as we have grown in conscious awareness through our diverse set of personal experiences on Earth. She has served as a battleground and tempering zone, the zone used to evolve us from lower-density unaware creatures to higher 5th-dimensional self-aware beings – but her purpose does not end there.

Mother Earth, our beautiful Gaia, is alive (remember, she could not produce life if she herself was not alive), and as a sentient being, she is also ascending to higher dimensions. She is to be the home of our New Earth, where Camelot, the Golden Age, The Age of Aquarius, Heaven on Earth will manifest through the actions inspired by our Divine awareness.

The Bible speaks clearly of this "new earth."

Isaiah 65:17:

"For behold, I create new heavens and a new earth; and the former things will not be remembered or come to mind."

We are actively in the process of creating such a Heaven on Earth...right here, right now. People from every culture all over the world are aware of these dynamics, their awareness heightened by epic myths and stories about these times. Some of the more enlightened humans among us (lightworkers) are now bringing forth this information through multiple channels of communication to awaken and help enlighten others.

It's no coincidence that digital technology, computers, and the Internet exploded at the same time we are experiencing a major consciousness shift. The Internet is serving to expand mass consciousness. It is a tool used by Love to bring us out of lower-density/dimensional thinking into the Unity and Love of 5th dimensional thinking.

In this day-and-age of instant information, every inquiry is answered in a flash using digital technology. Smartphones, tablets, smart-watches and computers are all powerful tools that contribute to the acceleration of these times, to the "quickening." *There is little wait time for information anymore.*

These tools have always been part of the plan...to enable people to explore and discover these new possibilities. Receiving instant answers to the questions that logical minds are asking paves the way to understanding and accepting this new way of living, of being.

That's what this consciousness shift is about. When enough people raise their consciousness to that of Cosmic Consciousness/Christ Consciousness, when mass consciousness is no longer about war but about Love, when we've reached critical mass with that feeling, knowing and being, then we will see the outer manifestation of our "Golden City of Light" of the New Camelot manifest upon Mother Earth.

"Merlin's playground of magical creation will manifest again, more glorious than ever. Its time is now."

In the past, these changes have come very slowly as humanity laboriously progressed to its present level of awareness. However, be aware that the end of cosmic cycles we discussed earlier, and ready access to information via the Internet accelerates the process. This newly harnessed electromagnetic energy arriving from the Cosmos is shifting us rapidly, much quicker than before, and that is why it's called the *"quickening."*

Ephesians 2:1 tells us that *"we are by nature spiritually dead, and that when the miracle of the New Birth takes place, we are born again by the quickening work of the Holy Spirit."*

We are being tuned and aligned to harmonize with the Symphony of Love, the Music of the Spheres, the Unity-Verse, *our authentic frequency.* It is an electromagnetic shifting of our consciousness, our vibration, our frequency, our awareness, our understanding and expression of Love.

This evolved consciousness is empowered to join our dueling sides, the male and female energy, the intuition and the logic, into one Creative Force/dance in service to Divine Will; heart and mind joined in Divine Unity of inspired thought and action on Earth as it is in heaven.

What a sacred and beautiful dance it is! *We become the mind of God/Source creating in the physical/material world.*

Male energy is electric (it gives) and female energy is magnetic (it receives). We are both male and female, a combination of electric and magnetic forces, and these forces are at battle in our minds until *cosmic awareness joins the two together in Unity for One purpose.*

This is the sacred alchemical marriage of bride and groom/female and male, intuition and logic, body and soul, Earth and heaven, matter and spirit, *joined in service to the One* – the Source, Love.

It is the creation of the Divine Human as male and female energies join in ecstatic conscious creation rather than ignorant competitive destruction.

Rather than running off to some supposed heaven of the future, leaving Mother Earth in ruins, how about we join hands with her to create a Divine Human and a Divine utopia right here on Earth?

Believe me, you don't want to leave now! The real fun has only just begun! We have recently reached the most magical aspect of creation, *conscious creation,* in which we can consciously participate with creation because our awareness has aligned with Source, with Love.

Magic occurs when our mind of logic and our heart of intuition become One in service to Love. When our masculine and feminine energies work as one, toward one end, we become the conscious creators we were created to be!

This magic carpet ride has just begun. So, hang on!

As this higher perception of life, this clearer understanding and clarity of Love reveals itself to receptive channels, we are becoming as children again, full of wonder, joy, awe, surprise, discovery, excitement, and laughter. Children laugh at the simplest of things; they find joy in the simplest of things.

We are remembering our connection to Source and waking from deep slumber (think "Sleeping Beauty). *Kissed by Love*, we've awakened to embrace and express our Divine attributes here on Earth, and *"live happily ever after!"*

    We are the fairy tale.

The Intuition

"There is a light that shines beyond all things on Earth, beyond all of us, beyond the heavens, beyond the highest, the very highest heavens. This is the light that shines in our heart."

– Chandogya Upanishad

12

Heart-Conscious Creation

It is no coincidence that the symbol for Love, for Source energy, is a heart. *The heart is the first organ to develop in the womb.* Your heart rules; it contains the perfect blueprint of Love for you.

Your brain comes later, after the development of the tongue and lungs. Your brain answers to your heart, not the other way around. Without that initial heartbeat, that vibration, that frequency of YOU, there is no brain. The brain develops because the heart does; therefore, it is subject to the heart.

Studies at the Institute for HeartMath discovered that the heart, not the brain, is the center of electromagnetic activity within us. There are 100 times more electrical signals being sent out from the heart than the brain, and 5,000 more magnetic signals. The brain is more of a receiving, interpreting, and sending station, a tool, but the heart is the original source/ operator.

After all, it came before all the others and, as the first organ created, it is directly connected to Source.

We are moving out of our minds into heart-conscious creating, where things begin. We are moving into the natural flow of life and creation without the subconscious mind's straitjacket of personal limits and beliefs (all created from fear/survival/ protection mode).

In this new paradigm we think with the Heart, the Sacred Heart/the Immaculate Heart of higher intuitive feelings. The Sacred Heart of Jesus and the Immaculate Heart of Mary are represented in so many religions and faiths. There are thousands of visual examples to admire.

The painting shown here is titled: *Sacred Heart of Jesus,* by José María Ibarrarán y Ponce , created in 1896. *The finger is clearly pointing to the heart.*

It is the heart that holds the answers we are looking for, not the mind.

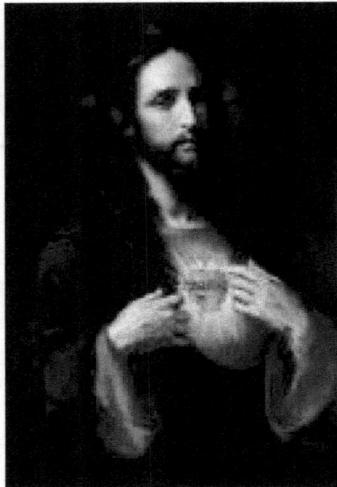

The key, the direct path to the heart, is to be present in the moment just as a child is. It is to experience the joy of life in complete union with the moment and your outer physical senses, while your inner intuitive senses play with magic creating more joy for you to experience through the realization of your dreams in the outer world.

What would be the purpose of creating your passions, your beautiful dreams and visions in physicality, if you did not have physical senses to enjoy them with?

It is a grand cycle. You get full enjoyment of your physical senses (no one could ever convince me that the intoxicating smell of a rose is not meant to be enjoyed) without the interruption of personal opinion (you've cleaned out all your head trash; your subconscious rubbish/rules) so more of what you want is constantly appearing in your present because your inner intuitive senses are free to create *without the conditions of your subconscious mind limiting, distorting and sabotaging them.*

I suggest you read that again.

Both the inner and outer senses have an exquisitely Divine purpose, and when working in unison, are a harmonious blend of magic and Love.

"When the individual is able to enter a world in which the two aspects of yin and yang return to their original unity, the mission of these two symbols comes to an end." Masanobu Fukuoka

Your inner senses are magnetically connected to your heart. They are your higher-tuned senses. They are the ones that guide you through life, intuitively revealing all your heart's desires – your divinely perfect path.

Your outer senses function through the electrical circuitry in your brain. Your inner senses are governed by the magnetic circuitry of your heart. They were created to work together, and we've finally evolved far enough to *consciously* do that.

Most people can't, or don't, enjoy their outer senses for the purpose they were created because they are off in the past or future of their minds, creating dramas rather than "stopping to smell the roses." There is no time to stop and smell roses when they are off in their minds trying to figure out how to pay next month's bills.

They experience the weeds of anxiety, stress, and disempowerment as opposed to the blossoms and beauty of the sensual present, where action, self-realization, and empowerment are met.

Conversely, there are those who get so enamored with their just-discovered inner realm that they get caught up in the idea of higher intuitive senses (the ones related to Spirit) and give little attention to the physical ones (those related to matter), as if they no longer held any importance.

This creates another split because they were created to work together for the full enjoyment of life, not separately. It is the separation – the experience of one without the other – that has caused our distorted beliefs, opinions, and perceptions and the resultant disease, depression and death.

The sleep state occurred when we got so caught up in our outer senses (trying to survive) that we plum forgot about our inner senses! Eventually the outer senses became our master, overshadowing and dulling our inner senses. (All in the grand plan, of course.)

You can see this process at work in the development of children. Children are so connected to magic and wonder when they are very young! As the poet Wordsworth put it, "trailing clouds of glory do we come from God, who is our home." Unguarded and wide open to experience, some of these cloud-trailing newcomers even speak with fairies and have fun with secret friends. Indeed, as the poet continues, "Heaven lies about us in our infancy!" But as they grow and encounter more of the outer world, and more of the world's opinions begin to *shape their perceptions* of the way things should be, *this magical essence fades,* and into the "prison-house" goes the spirit. ("Intimations of Immortality," William Wordsworth)

The subconscious is like a lump of clay being molded and shaped during infancy and early childhood. This programming becomes our operating system and defines how we behave and our purpose in life. In other words, it becomes our reality and identity going forward.

In 2006, the Spitzer Space Telescope took pictures of an amazing nebula that had formed *very near our galactic center.* Now, everyone knows there are "billions and billions" (thank you, Carl Sagan) of stars and galaxies in the Universe, so what's so special about that?

It is the first time anyone has seen one shaped like a *double helix.*

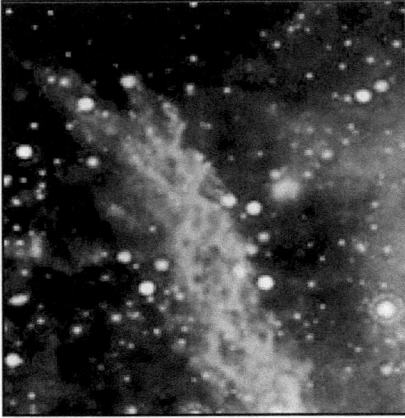

"Nobody has ever seen anything like that before in the cosmic realm. Most nebulae are either spiral galaxies full of stars or formless amorphous conglomerations of dust and gas — space weather. What we see indicates a high degree of order." – NASA

What is a double helix? DNA is a double helix. As our DNA connects and awakens with this new powerful energy (all attention is now on understanding and decoding our DNA), our conscious understanding and clarity of Love shifts into a higher resonance, as is reflected in this *ordered nebula.*

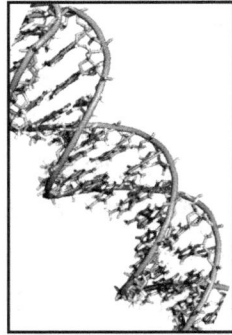

A stunning representation of the Universal Law "As above, so below," we have before us a heavenly reflection of what is happening to all beings here on Earth. Focus is on DNA.

Everything is really right in front of our eyes *if we are paying attention.*

The mind was designed to be used in harmonious cooperation with the heart's desires and is presently being tempered to express Divine Will on Earth. For most people the mind is the master, the ruler, and a tyrant, while the heart has become its servant. That's what we're about to change.

Once we've exhausted the search for life's satisfactions and solutions outside of ourselves, and earnestly begin our search for empowered responses to life's challenges and ills within ourselves, we discover that all the answers were literally "right under our nose." (It's interesting to note here that the brain is above the nose, but the heart is under the nose; the heart holds the answers.) Clarity was possible all along, but we never looked.

This is not about beating down the subconscious (after all, everything that is created has a divine purpose); it's about embracing the deep-rooted fears that developed when we were trying to survive, and reprogramming this distorted subconscious energy into Love.

We are moving out of fear and into Love. Fear splits one into two (cause and effect); Love joins two as one.

No longer will we experience a split in what our mind wants and what our heart desires. Minds and hearts will work in unison, becoming one – vibrating to one Harmony, one frequency, the Unity-Verse, Love.

The heart creates spontaneously in the moment while the mind creates threats, situations, and dramas to fill with energy. Just think what an honorable partner the subconscious will be when it is operating from Love. Once its data has been updated to Love programming rather than fear and cooperation replaces competition.

The shape of a heart is not accidental. It represents the joining of two sides, the intuitive and logical sides, until they are perfectly balanced, aligned and working as a team.

It is the consciousness of Unity, of Love.

Heart-conscious creation is inspired creation; it occurs *when the heart speaks to the mind. Not the other way around.* But the mind must be open to receive and quiet enough to hear. Trying to hear Truth, trying to hear Love speaking through a mind full of "head trash," is like trying to hear a cell phone message with a static connection. There is simply too much interference.

A mind filled with head trash/distorted perceptions (static) would not hear what the heart was trying to tell it, and whatever it did hear would be *badly distorted.*

However, a mind that has been cleansed and scoured of all negative residues, of all subconscious fears, the mind that works in balanced Unity of purpose rather than divided by cause and effect, becomes the sparkling vehicle through which the Divine may manifest without distortions. When this happens, the heart speaks to the mind and they work together to realize our desires without the intrusion of old programming.

They work together to create magic.

According to Gnostic teachings:

"The power of the heart is intuition, the ability to know without reasoning, just to know it. It is a type of knowledge that is far beyond the intellect; it is Divine. With intuition, we can navigate the most difficult and complex problems with utter simplicity, because we

do not have to think about them. We do not reason, we do not compare options, we do not analyze, we just know."

Rumi expressed it a bit more poetically:

"Put your thoughts to sleep; do not let them cast a shadow over the moon of your heart. Let go of thinking."

Personal thought is a product of our confused and contaminated subconscious mind, whereas inspired thought is a product of our uncontaminated hearts.

We must stand in our power as conscious creators, transmuting energy from one state to another by the focus and warmth of conscious intended Love. (Reflect on the ice, water, and steam metaphor.) We must work in conjunction and alignment with the single source of creation, Love.

When we're caught up in the joy of the moment and literally "plugged into" power, into Source, into Love, brilliant intuitive thoughts come blazing through. It's as if they appear from nowhere, but the reality is, we've *simply plugged in.* That's when serendipity and synchronicity dance with spontaneous, joyous, abandon.

And, the irony and paradox of it all is this: In order to plug in, we must let go.

For example, just as I am writing this book, the inspiration comes for the cover. I now know exactly what I want on the cover because it revealed itself to me *when I was not thinking about it!* It came out of nowhere, and the minute it appeared in my inner vision I knew that was it.

These inspired thoughts spring from the intentions of the heart, not the mind; they are always in alignment with our most perfect expression. They are the voice of Divine Love/Will expressing through us, but we must be tuned in, so we recognize them when they appear.

The mind (without input from the heart) operates from the subconscious and only draws upon the results and feelings of past experiences. It relies solely on past programming, all dictated by fear (remember, that's all it knows). The heart, because it is the first organ created, springs directly from Love. It dwells in Unity of one power, one Source; it operates in the moment and knows only Love.

These times are about living spontaneously and playfully creating in the present, without the opinions and biases of the fearful subconscious mind getting in the way! We cannot live spontaneously if we are lost in our thoughts. That's when we are busy creating new dramas out of old subconscious files.

This new energy is about magic, and magic has nothing to do with work! Magic happens when we are not thinking. It's when we let go of the so-called problem that the inspired solution appears. If thinking had anything to do with magic, we'd have a world overrun with magicians right now. But the opposite is true. People know anything but magic.

It is thinking we must let go of if we are to play with magic. If we want to "plug in" and allow Love to express through us then we must remove and transmute any thoughts that are out of alignment with Love, that block the flow of Love.

All fears and their "groupies" must go. That means guilt, judgments, anxiety, stress, jealousy, resentment, anger, doubt – you know the ones I'm talking about. Anything that exists and thrives in a polarized world must go.

Drop your personal opinions and get out of your dueling thoughts and into the present moment where Love lives and expresses. Move into Heart Intelligence, the expression of Love, whose purpose is to create/manifest in line with Divine Will in the moment "on earth as it is in heaven."

Literally quit thinking (shut down the dialogue in your head, all of it) and allow your higher intuitive Heart-Centered Intelligence to come through.

That's when the magic begins.

....

You must learn to "think with the heart
and love with the mind."

....

The Innocence

"The wisest you have ever been as human beings is when you were little children. They are so uninhibited and joyful...they are authentic."

– Dr. Bruce Lipton

13

As Simple as Child's Play

Excitement is an element...an attribute of the present moment, of the new, of the now, of discovery and revelation.

How easy is that to understand? I told you it would be as simple as child's play. After all, didn't Master Jesus once say that you must become as little children before you can enter the Kingdom of Heaven?

Remember the flaming "open heart?" He is pointing us to the magic! He is pointing to the Heart, where magic reveals itself to our conscious understanding.

The way to magic, to the 5th dimension, is shown by children. We need to become as children again.

Children don't work, they play. They imagine, they see no borders, boundaries, or limitations. They love to participate, experience and discover! This is before their purity is sullied by their conditioning, and their little minds get contaminated with fear.

They are perfect examples of living in the moment, consciously participating in life and letting *Joy* bubble up spontaneously, *without getting in its way.* They are joyful because they live in the moment where joy is experienced. They do not worry about the future, nor are they obsessed with the past. They are totally authentically absorbed in the moment and all the excitement that it offers.

Children believe that anything is possible (until they are told that it isn't). They are full of wonder and the awe of discovery, taking delight in simple things like the taste of a new ice-cream flavor or the simple joy of being read to before bedtime.

When was the last time you enjoyed a new flavor of ice cream without "getting in the way" of your enjoyment, by entertaining a negative aspect, such as "This will make me fat," or "I'm so weak I just can't seem to stick to my diet?" Even if you're thin, it might occur to you that the cone is overpriced, is too large or too small, is a cheap brand, is too filling . . . An overactive negative imagination can make any harmless treat, or experience, something to fear or be leery of. But for the child, it's simply .... *Yummy!*

What negative labels do you automatically attach to things? What definitions and thoughts do *you* harbor? You know them well because they hang out with you, just waiting for that opening, that moment to express. They are constantly berating you and others. Usually after your initial excitement

– let's say, at the first spoonful of your favorite dessert those Negative Nellie subconscious "groupies" come rushing in to ruin the moment with their fear and guilt.

A child feels none of that. Pure and simple, their happy excitement begins the moment they step through the door of the shop and continues as the ice cream arrives and they take their first lick…and lasts all the way through to their final crunch. Their joy has not been disturbed by labels, judgments, or any kind of reservation. They don't entertain fearful subconscious beliefs and definitions that rob them of their joy.

In fact, a child's excitement grows in anticipation, and they are not afraid to show it. They exude joy because they are living in the moment, allowing Divine essence to express without "shadows of doubt."

For them, *there is no cause having an effect;* there is simply the excitement of the moment, and they are not afraid to show their enjoyment authentically.

That's the magic that children embody, and it's why we love to watch them so much. It's their innocent Love and expression of *authentic joy* that attracts us and for a moment in time, allows us to experience the same kind of bliss.

As an adult, you look at that ice cream and see the cause of your weight before you even take a bite. (That's the kind of *perception* I've been talking about.) It's not the ice cream making you suffer...*It's your preconceived guilt, your perception – your definition of the moment, your label of "fat,"* before you even take that first bite. It's the weight of this anxiety and the vision in your head that *causes* your weight gain.

"As a man thinketh in his heart, so is he." Proverbs 23:7

The ice cream is an innocent bystander. (Your logic should tell you that if ice cream were the true culprit, then everyone who ate ice cream would be fat, which is obviously untrue.) If you continue to point fingers at the ice cream as the cause, your weight will respond with the expected effect, because that is what you are in the moment. *How can you express anything other than what you consciously are? They are one and the same thing.*

Children don't worry about these things. They are not anxious; they do not spend their time worrying and fussing about an imagined future. Nor are they saddled with guilt about the cause and effect of things from the past. Not until their consciousness gets colored and conditioned by the world's view do fearful habits of thought and behavior emerge.

Until then, they are a clean slate...in receptive, allowing, discovering mode. Come on in, Universe, and show me your goods, all of them! I want to experience it all! That is the mind of a child, the kind of mind that you would do well to embrace if experiencing heaven is important to you.

Heaven is right here...right now. It is a state of consciousness that is waiting for your acceptance and expression now, not in some imaginary future. There is no judgment keeping you out of heaven except your own. It is your perceptions, your personal views, judgments, beliefs, and opinions, that are blocking your view of heaven, nothing else. You need to adjust your perceptions (your frequency) to express (to resonate with) the Unity-Verse, the powerful vibrating frequency of all-inclusive Love.

This is the Love that leaves nothing out and does not entertain a limited view of the world.

Creation is magical – just ask any child. But we can't connect with it, we can't plug in if our personal agendas are getting in the way, continually trying to convince us that we must work to create and filling our minds with old agendas to do it with.

Those are rules of survival, fear, and lower-frequency duality thinking and creating. But remember – we're consciously moving out of time: past and future (3D/4D) to the present/now (5D), and *our gift for giving the Universe our presence (our awareness) is the magic of playful creation in the present.*

We tend to ignore the present moment (the only real energy there is) and exchange it for trips into our anxious future as we try to figure out/project our life, or we exchange this present energy for glimpses into the past, which usually result in our minds dwelling in negative thoughts, opinionated or judgmental, especially against ourselves.

These kinds of thoughts keep us locked in survival mode. They keep us reaching for something in the future as if we don't have access to everything right now, or worse, *blaming and judging ourselves for actions of the past.*

Is that how a young child behaves? Are they constantly in their minds, stressing about paying bills or berating themselves for past actions? No! But I bet you do, *just as I used to before I found the "magic!"*

Either way, these kinds of thoughts signal that energy needs transmuting because Love is not being *consciously* felt or expressed. Love is always there (remember, Love is Source energy) but if we don't consciously "see" Love (if our perceptions are giving us a distorted view) then we will not have the experience of Love because we are not consciously plugged into Love.

A child, on the other hand, is consciously plugged into the moment, into the magic, into Love. They are authentic and not afraid to express themselves. This authentic alignment, *this authentic love of who they are,* keeps the channels clean, unclogged, and freely flowing with life energy...with chi, the vital force that keeps us alive.

The body is an amazing bioelectrical system. All glands,

organs, meridians, nodes – all systems work as one unit. It is a working system...parts do not operate independently. When we live authentically, in alignment with Love, our chakras are spinning correctly and aligned and our bioenergetic systems are tuned and humming as well.

Energetic disturbances happen as we begin trying to please others for the sake of their acceptance rather than just being authentic and loving who we are and owning the feelings we are experiencing. Everything we feel is valid and needs to be owned, and when we do not own it, we create a blockage of energy. Young children (before they are programmed) own what they are and express it without fear. They are authentic to themselves.

Remove the dams you've erected in your energy signature by claiming and loving all that you are. Claim yourself, honor yourself, be yourself. Fall in love with yourself "because of who you are," not "despite who you are."

Honoring yourself is the greatest form of gratitude you can express and the highest form of Love you can give.

Each time you do not express your authentic self you hide behind yet another "veil," you cover yourself up, you are ashamed of who you are.

Think of the Adam and Eve story, and how they covered themselves up when they no longer felt their connection to Source/Unity...to Love.

For the first time, they felt shame and covered themselves. How many times have you felt shame because of your disconnect with Source?

Bottling your real feelings and expressing inauthentic feelings to please others creates a distinct distortion in frequency...a blockage of energy (your chi life force energy) that needs to flow freely through all channels and systems of your body if you are to stay balanced, healthy, and harmonious.

Listening and following a pre-programmed mind invites disaster into our lives. These fearful ideas bring discomfort, sadness, and ill health, yet most people just can't figure out how to turn their lives around and get out of this self-defeating programming. It's how they've been operating for as long as they remember, and they simply don't know any other way to live. It's their way of survival, it's what they know. It's their comfort zone.

It's always scary to peek out from one's comfort zone. But isn't that where the excitement is? How can you continually feel excitement about past experiences? Excitement is all about discovery, the venturing forth, the pulling back of the veils, the journeying into the unknown that ignites passion.

Excitement is an element, an attribute of the present moment, of the new, of the now. It's the feeling young children have when they wake in the morning, ready to embrace and discover more of life.

You can't feel excited in the past, nor can you feel excited in the future; however, you can feel excited in the moment – without limits! "But wait," you may say. I do feel excitement about the future. *Yes, but the excitement is felt in the moment, the excitement is felt now, not in some supposed future.*

Creation starts perfectly in the heart (remember, our hearts are always telling us what is best for us because they are directly connected directly to Source) but the message gets distorted when it is received by a mind ruled by fear. If we keep our minds anchored and focused in the moment (as a child does), there is no distortion to the message and creation comes through clear, pure, and magical!

When you align with Divine Will, which you only "hear" when all the dialogue in your head has been silenced – and no, you can't keep some voices and expel others (you might just call it bankruptcy of the mind) – you align with synchronicity, serendipity, spontaneity, and Unity; they become your daily playmates.

A caterpillar cannot become a butterfly by refusing to molt, by holding onto its old skin and energy pattern of being a caterpillar. It must willingly relinquish what it is/its present purpose and allow a higher purpose to emerge. This will all seem like magic compared to our previous life of work and toil but is the way we were created to live – the way we were created to CREATE!

We are what we see. *Our world is formed from our perceptions* – we see what our perceptions are telling us to see. If we are suffering in any way it is because our present perceptions are formed from old programming, the old stories and dramas that belong to us alone.

We are hanging onto fear, playing victim and honoring two forces. Seen as "good and bad," their results dutifully appear in our world.

Living in a mind of dueling forces is like living in a perpetual war. A war you can never win.

We have cycled through another 24,000 years and are now experiencing a cosmic solar birthday. We are being invited into the secrets of the Universe as this Light-filled expanded Love energy arrives, awakens and enlightens us, raising our frequency and expanding our consciousness. This new energy is refining our DNA, stripping off our veils, shifting our electromagnetic energy, and releasing the Light from within.

We are evolving and experiencing a giant leap in consciousness/in our understanding, clarity, and expression of Love. We are becoming both *receivers and generators of Light*. As more and more people align with this energy and release old subconscious patterns and programs (distrust, protection, vulnerability, and survival programming), transmuting them with Love energy, the world about us will increasingly reflect this new way of thinking, this Heaven on Earth, our new Camelot.

We are Grand Alchemists with the power to move and transmute energy by the focus of our attention/intention – "Let there be Light" – command. When we focus as Love, the most potent energy in the Universe, we transmute lower, dense frequencies into the finer, higher, and lighter frequencies of Love.

We are Love in action as we tune in, harmonize, and weave Love frequencies together.

A little summary of the previous chapters:

We are energy.

Energy is the essence within all things; all things are a form of energy. Energy is manipulated and changed/transformed by intent and focus (consciousness).

The Heart is the first organ created and holds within it the perfect blueprint of who we are. It is our direct connection to Love, to Source.

Inspired intent and focus are created in the Heart.

Polarized intent and focus are created in the personal, opinionated, dual mind.

The untrained/sullied mind creates from fear; the Heart creates from and only knows Love, because it is Love.

All things work together for good to those who Love God, for God is what all things are. To love God means to move into alignment with our One true vibration, our authentic vibration...Love.

When we are aligned with our one true vibration/self, we are harmonized; we are in harmony and we experience all things in harmony. When we are not aligned with our One true self, we experience discord because we are out of harmony with the whole...with the oneness of what we authentically are. These distortions in our vibratory pattern eventually manifest as discord, dis-ease and unhappiness.

- 3D is the dimension of fear and preoccupation with survival, of victimhood, of two minds/ two powers, the good - the bad, the caterpillar, the ice, and the perpetual war. It is the polarized world.

- 4D is the rainbow bridge to the dimensions of Higher Consciousness. As we expand our conscious understanding of Love and express it more and more freely, we move up (expand) in consciousness. Tempered in 4D, we finally arrive with full understanding and clarity in the 5th dimension. The 4th dimension serves as the transition cycle – old to new…the chrysalis of the caterpillar.

- 5D is Unity of purpose. In Unity consciousness we see beyond the outer effects of fear to the inner radiance of Love. We know, see, and experience only Love because we have eliminated from our subconscious any residue of patterns that were not in harmony with Love. We are in tune and harmonized with the Unity-Verse (the Universe). We have developed "eyes that see and ears that hear."

By law you only "see" what you resonate with (what your perceptions allow you to believe). Otherwise, you would not recognize it.

Unity/Singularity is the starting point; all division springs from this and eventually returns to it.

One will always come before two.

The Friction

"Your task is not to seek for love, but merely to seek and find all barriers within yourself that you have built against it."

– Rumi

14

Recognizing Resistance

How do we go from being a caterpillar to a butterfly? How are we reborn as innocent children, free from our distorted views? How do we recognize resistance?

Recognizing what resistance does in our lives becomes easy when we fully accept the *Law of Resistance.*

Workout buffs know the truth of resistance because they apply this law every time they work out to achieve their finely tuned muscular strength. Muscles respond to resistance by growing larger. It is the resistance applied in strength training that builds muscle.

It is law. *Whatever you resist, persists.* Not only does it persist, but it grows larger commensurate with the energy you focus into it.

Apply a lot of pressure...apply a lot of resistance to any given situation and you can literally turn a molehill into a mountain. How many times have you done this in your life and then reflected on the mess you made of things because you were playing the victim role rather than taking responsibility for what appeared by assuming the alchemist role?

When we apply false labels to things and conditions that appear in our lives (based upon our distorted perceptions) and believe that something outside of us is responsible for the occurrence, we assume the victim role and assign power to these conditions and circumstances, as though they have some sort of control in our lives.

We give our power to whatever it is we are blaming for the circumstance. After all, we are saying that something had power "over" us, that something beyond our control was responsible for our condition. We have given our power away to this "something."

How disempowering is that?

Resistance is the result of focusing energy on what you don't want. Fearful focus and attention on negative aspects of your life – on the things you don't like – are manifesting more of the same for you because your frequency is magnetically aligned with that frequency. Your energy is feeding and growing it and your observations and skewed perceptions are shaping and molding it.

You cannot express in your life anything that you are not in frequency alignment with. How could you? If your frequency is aligned with fear, doubt, anger, etc., how do you expect to manifest Peace, Joy, and Love?

Your energy signature, your frequency, is your expression. They are one and the same. It is what you are now, and what you are now is the only reality. The rest lives in your mind.

Get a grip on your mind and out of the opinionated, personal, fear-laced thoughts dictating your life and actions and into alignment with infinite Love and all possibility. You are at the controls. You just need to exercise them.

All possibility has always existed to us, but our minds have limited access to it because they are out of frequency alignment with our true authentic vibration, that of Love, and more in alignment with fear.

Just as a caterpillar must willingly let go of being a caterpillar to become a butterfly (can you imagine a caterpillar resisting change?), so too must we willingly let go of our energetic patterns that are out of alignment with Love/Divine Will if we wish to transform into the new.

What would happen to a caterpillar that resisted change? It would die as a caterpillar and never reach the freedom, euphoria, and exhilaration of becoming a butterfly.

Sound familiar?

That's how our lives have played out in previous incarnations. But remember, these are special times we're in; we've just completed a 24,000-year cycle of consciousness growth. The veils covering our conscious understanding are thinning, and anyone whose heart, mind, soul, and strength are focused on Oneness and Unity, with Love, shall be freed from the tyranny of the fear-programmed subconscious mind.

How then do we identify and rid ourselves of these veils, of this darkness that overshadows our Light, keeping us from the 5th dimension? We must be able to target this distorted energy (resistance) as it surfaces if we are to consciously change and transmute it to a higher, expanded expression of Love energy – and begin to magically create.

The process is simple and there is no need for long philosophical or psychological explanations. If you feel you need or want such constructs, there are plenty of incredible sources online that will keep your mind busy for a long time. There is a path for everyone who seeks.

However, this is a book about simplicity and ease!

The complicated processes, the ensnaring words, hidden meanings, and definitions are anachronisms. This is about the new way of seeing and doing, and the new is about returning to the innocence of a child's mind. It's about playing with magic, and has nothing to do with work, scientific or theological terminology, or psychological analyses!

If we are to be as children again, what in the world could a child understand about that?

Children respond to Love, and that is our first clue to becoming children again.

Have a heart and mind full of Love. See Love in everything you observe. It's so simple, yet we've made it so complicated. Align your consciousness with the power of Love. See the energy of Love all around you before your personal labels get attached to things. See and be Love in the way of a newborn babe, still awash in it, the mind pure and unclouded. Become that innocent child again. Move out of your polarized world of duality, definitions, limiting labels and comparisons into the Unity of Love.

Bring all that is essentially you into the Light, into the "command" of Love. It really is that simple.

Simplicity speaks directly to the heart, while things too complicated speak only to the intellect.

Be the so-called tabula rasa (blank slate) of a newborn babe and take in life through untainted, unbiased eyes, free of resistance. When you do, the wonder and awe of life's journey – the excitement and discovery – return to everything you see, say and do.

The amazing thing is that you are viewing the same world you were viewing a few seconds ago, when you embraced duality and fear. The world has not changed one bit but your *perception* of it has!

When you begin taking bites out of life with the enthusiasm and heart of a child (free of resistance), something magical takes place: you connect with the original source of Love and the innocence and magic of creation.

A child is born with a heart of Love, not fear. Love is born and raised in the heart, while fear is born and raised in the mind.

Remember, the heart knows of your needs before your mind does because the heart is your direct frequency connection to Love. Your mind serves as the interpreter, and if it is distorted from unresolved fears coloring your view, then guess what? The original blueprint sent from the heart gets blurred by energy that is out of alignment with the higher frequency of Love and your life reflects these distorted perceptions.

When you are energetically aligned with the moment, impulses from the heart come in synchronous surprises because there are no distorted thoughts causing resistance and blocking the flow of this divine energy.

These blockages, and veils are thought-patterns and beliefs that label things as being outside of Love, leaving illusions in your mind that warp your perceptions of life.

As you begin to understand that everything appearing in your life reflects your perceptions, then you quit playing the victim role and own what appears. You move out of resistance and take responsibility. There is no judgment attached because you understand that all disturbances of energy were created when you were frightened, when your consciousness did not yet know itself as Love and was hiding behind its "fear/protective files." Be gentle with yourself. You did not know any other way.

It's easy to own this energy when you understand there is no judgment attached to it.

Harmony is the result of aligning and harmonizing all feelings, thoughts, words, and actions with your authentic frequency – that of Love. When every note you play in life is in perfect harmony with the Symphony of Love, you are tuned into the Unity-Verse…the Universal song of creation, the Uni-verse – *U-in-verse.*

The opposite is disharmony and discordant music (your life).

That's it in a nutshell. The simpler you keep things, the closer to Truth you are.

The Dance

*The opposites give definition,
and Knowledge comes from
direct experience.*

15

You Can't Have One Without the Other

Opposites/complements are needed to manifest form. What is cold without hot to gauge it against? They are at opposite ends of the frequency scale, but they are complementary and of the same substance, the original Source. *Each one gives form, expression, and definition to the other.*

You are both the creator and creation. The creator has no purpose or existence without creation and creation has no existence without a creator. You can't have one without the other.

The play of opposites never goes away...it is perceptions that change. Your perceptions can warp your world with fears or create a Heaven on Earth with Love.

Wise Teachers, Sages and Masters walk the same earth and ride the same ebb and flow of life that we do, with one major difference. In all moments, their perceptions are in line with Love, so, the only thing they experience is Love. Their frequency is aligned, in harmony and resonating with the rhythm of the Universe.

Love is theirs in every moment for no other reason than the fact that they claim it as theirs by BEING IT.

Fear is used by Love to bring us to an awareness and appreciation of Love. You simply can't know Love without having known fear first. You would have no appreciation or knowledge of what Love is. And when you abide fully in Love, you are empowered to express magic.

Love is all things when we operate from Unity consciousness, and we need to ditch the labels our personal thoughts/programs want to attach to things. Rather, we must accept *life's dual expression as Love's way of becoming self-conscious...conscious of itself as Love.*

We need to accept the truth that negative is as essential as positive. Without negative, positive has no value, no meaning, and vice versa. They each give definition to the other, therefore, neither can exist without the other.

Can Light be created without electricity and magnetism? Light is an electromagnetic wave. The two forces, electricity and magnetism (male and female), *working as one force, create Light.*

Do you see? The Light within us is the same. To create/ BE Light you must consciously be balanced between male/ logical/electrical energy and female/intuitive/magnetic energy.

When you consciously join these two forces within you, they work together for *One Purpose, to create LIGHT.*

A new higher-frequency consciousness is born of this union – a higher mind, the Light of Christ, the Christ Mind.

Just as electricity joins with magnetism to create LIGHT in the physical realm, the same rules apply to your inner world. Your male and female sides, the electric and magnetic, must be joined and balanced completely if you want to BE LIGHT.

Male and female energy – the electric and magnetic, intellect and intuition, mind and heart, heaven and Earth, spirit and matter – joined together in Love – create the Divine Child, Christ Consciousness. *Consciousness with full awareness of being Divine in nature.*

I repeat, "living under two powers that are in constant battle is a war you can never win." There is only Unity, Source, and Love expressing as opposite poles. It is the dance of complementary opposites, the dance of life. Anything else is a creation of your personal mind and belongs to you alone. There is nothing that is not Love and perfect in its own time. It is your perceptions, your labels, that are less than Loving, less than perfect.

It is all done in, through, and by Love for Love.

"When you disengage from battle there is no battle, not for you." Merlin

The difficult conditions we experience as we navigate through life often appear toxic and detrimental because of the immediate pain and discomfort we feel. However, they offer the greatest opportunity for growth, learning, and mind expansion. It is all part of our metamorphosis and the growth of Love within us, so that we can express and expand this Love without.

Just as heat/fire is used to cure impurities in the physical world, so too is this process used to cure impurities in the inner spiritual world/consciousness. The heat that's generated from the friction of third-and fourth-dimensional polarities burns off the dross of fear frequencies that cloud our perceptions. What's left is a radiant crystal light – a being of Love and Light.

The perfect diamond within – our crystal being, the purity of Love, *the essence of our authentic selves – the diamond in the lotus is revealed.* Just as carbon transforms over millions of years *under intense pressure* into the fullness of its potential – a beautiful radiant crystal diamond – so too do you have the potential to transform under intense pressure from carbon to crystal, from human to Divine.

Without "intense pressure," there is no diamond. It is the crystalline diamond that is left after the coal/carbon of our present bodies has been burned off by our experiences.

As the great Sufi poet Rumi expressed: *"If you are irritated by every rub, how do you expect to be polished?"*

It doesn't matter what you call it. You can label it xyz and it won't change the fact that all things spring from the same source, Unity, and all things work toward one purpose.

....

Butterfly, Butterfly,
When high in flight
Do you ever lament
the plight
of the Caterpillar
who came and went?
The Caterpillar
who gave its all
No knowledge
it had
of the coming event.
So, Butterfly
on your heavenly flight
pause to reflect
and give thanks
to the Caterpillar so bold
who altered its life
to follow its soul.

– Dr. Janni Lloyd

....

Womb of Transformation

When your desire to know yourself and your inner world becomes louder than your desire to experience more of the outer world, then you are ready for conscious cleansing.

16

The Chrysalis

Expressing a new state of expanded consciousness is the most rewarding thing you will ever do but requires commitment and disciplined attention to your thoughts, feelings, words, and actions.

First prerequisite: You must want it! Desire and commitment both play a huge role in your transformation because it's a matter of frequency alignment. It's your desire and commitment that focus the energy of your attention on the object or circumstance giving it the momentum to happen. Without focus, your energy is off creating something somewhere else.

If you are to free yourself of mind manipulation and become the Master of your life that you know you were created to be –

You must love "God" with all your heart, soul, mind, and strength. Only when your heart, soul, mind, and strength (thoughts, feelings, words and actions) are energetically unified in purpose are you ready to spin your chrysalis and make your transformation. This is the primary condition for moving forward.

Remember, this is about experiencing life as a child, one full of joy, excitement, enthusiasm, acceptance, and freedom. It's about exploring life as a young child does, free and clear of personal fears, limiting conditions and distorted perceptions.

It's about no longer hiding behind our carefully crafted personas to be loved and accepted. It's about being authentic, and in love with who we are as we are!

Sounds like fun, doesn't it? It is. Let's begin.

Whenever you want to clean out a container, the first thing you do, is shed light on the inside so that you can visibly "see" what needs cleaning! You are that container and Love is shining its Light deep inside you so that you are aware of what needs cleansing.

As you move forward in this process of clearing, the last and deepest wounds of negativity that will need healing are the judgments and the conditions you have placed on yourself. We somehow find it easier to forgive others but encounter difficulty in forgiving ourselves.

In other words, it's relatively easy to look outside oneself and love others despite their imperfections, as unconditionally loving parents routinely do. But, can you honestly say that you *love yourself,* despite your own many failures and flaws?

Can you honestly say that you love yourself without conditions?

My guess is that you are still deeply blaming and condemning yourself for the very things you wish to forgive in others.

But don't you see? That's the key to this whole "puzzle." You cannot forgive in others what you have not forgiven yourself for first. If the disturbing vibration (judgment of self) remains in you, unhealed and festering, you will continue to magnetically draw the same kinds of unforgiven people and circumstances that you are energizing within. It's the "Law of Resonance" at work.

It is this very subtle blaming and judging of yourself that causes you to see in others the qualities you do not like in yourself. You believe you have forgiven them but until you love yourself with complete acceptance and forgiveness, you can never give this love (this feeling) to others.

How can you give someone a frequency you do not own for yourself?

You magnetize to yourself the situations in life that address whatever it is you are judging in yourself. Whether condemning yourself for some real or imagined "sin," or congratulating yourself for some personal triumph, the rule is the same: You get what you give, because that is your frequency!

Life is your reflector mirror that enables you to see exactly what and who you are. Your life reflects all your thoughts, beliefs, and opinions, which have become your perceptions, and your perceptions are the tools of creation. How could it be otherwise?

You only recognize in others what exists in yourself... what matches your frequency, what you resonate with! Everything that comes into your life is being used by your Higher Self/Love to bring your attention to an area within YOU that needs healing, that needs "tuning" and aligning with your authentic vibration of Love. If you did not own this vibration within yourself, if you were not judging yourself for this condition, you would not recognize it as a failing in others because you would not resonate with it!

You must understand the vibration game. You "see" only what you resonate with because you are in frequency alignment with it. You are tuned into that "channel."

It bears repeating: *When you stop blaming and condemning yourself for things, then you no longer recognize these qualities in others.*

We cannot heal what we are not aware of. Whenever a negative reaction or response to an outer experience, person, place, or thing is felt, we can be certain there is distorted energy within us that needs transmuting/changing/shifting, and that is why it is being brought to our *conscious attention.*

This errant belief or energy pattern within our subconscious is a type of "shadow energy" or veil, created from a judgment or distorted perception we had in the past when our consciousness was out of alignment with Love and operating from survival/fear mode.

Your main job is to observe. It's really that simple. Get in front of your energy and become the disciplined observer of your life in all areas. Change reaction to controlled action and remain detached from the outcome, realizing that everything is a gift that works to bring you closer to and in alignment with Love.

Any discomfort and the recognition of negativity you feel is your first clue, your red-flag-waving that something needs to be healed, but the cause of the pain lies within your perceptions, beliefs, engrained energetic patterns, and opinions – your labels and titles for things, the thought patterns and programs that run on autopilot and control your life.

That's what needs to change. All thoughts, emotions, actions, and attitudes must align with Love, and there are no exceptions!

You can't grow Love by planting fear. You grow Love by planting/focusing on Love, by sowing the seeds of Love. Can you grow carrots by planting beans? Of course, not. You must plant the seeds of what you want to express, what you want to grow...what you want to see.

"Seeing evil" or negativity creates negative conditions in your life and circumstances because life becomes exactly what you "label" and "see" it to be. Your garden always blooms from the seeds that are planted.

What shows up in your outer world is all about you, and it always has been. How could it be about anyone else?

It is your world, your frequency, and you are creating it with your focused energy – your command of the Light. The key is to quit resisting the experiences that are not to your liking. They are all expressing for a reason, and that reason is the opportunity to cultivate conscious Love, as you choose Love over any lesser emotion or feeling. Period.

In the past, your circumstances and fears got the best of you. You pushed them away or did battle with them. Unaware of the Love behind them, you were judging yourself, and you were afraid, so, you resisted them and did anything but "own" them.

But these are magical times, no longer must you face those fears alone. Merlin has given us a tool, The Magic Wand of Light and Love, with its eternal life-giving powers of transmutation. Just one conscious wave of this wand transmutes fear and illusion to the reality of Love.

YOUR conscious focus on Love is that powerful tool!

Remember, Love is the vibration, the frequency of your authentic self. Neither you nor your footprint in life will be in harmony until you have brought all your energy into alignment with your authentic vibration...the frequency of Love.

There is no other way.

....

"And you shall love the Lord your God with all your heart, and
with all your soul, and with all your mind,
and with all your strength."
This is the first and greatest commandment.

....

The Magic

Alchemy: "The transformation of one type of energy-matter into another type of energy-matter."

17

Alchemy

There is nothing arcane or difficult to understand about this new way of doing things. We know that becoming a child again opens the gates to heaven, so we must follow in their footsteps if we are to consciously create Camelot and experience Heaven on Earth.

We must not allow our logic to complicate things but keep that free-flowing mind of a child open and receptive to what's coming our way. We must approach life with joy and feel the innocence of divine bliss and the beauty of rhythmic laughter and warm smiles as they burst forth spontaneously – *just as a child does.*

A child resides in the moment; they live in the moment where life HAPPENS - not in the mind where life is thought about.

We must venture forth into discovery, to experience and expand our awareness wherever that might lead us, without borders and barriers, condemnations or judgments, all driven by fear. We must quit trying to please others for the sake of acceptance and Love and realize that it is by being authentic that we align with Love and attract Love because we are Love!

Ok, so, let's have some fun…

Since Merlin is creatively behind this project, he has granted us the visual use of *magic wands*.

This will be the primary illumination you will use to navigate through all the dark and dense energy areas of your subconscious. Expect them to surface as you dig and shine your light into your vaults of deeply entrenched thoughts and fears, cleaning and clearing your vessel for ascension to the magical, wondrous world of fifth-dimensional innocence and Love.

Remember, lower density, duality driven thoughts do not resonate with 5th dimensional Love. These are all your fear-based thoughts, the ones that originated when you operated from survival and protection mode. You must clear your aura, your energy field, of this unneeded dialogue in your head before you are in total alignment with the resonating power of Love.

Now, imagine your wand. You can make this wand out of anything. Crystals, bark, wood, natural stone… give it the look *that your imagination is feeling*. Personalize it to your heart's content on your sparkling clean "imagination screen."

Now, place this wand you have *consciously crafted* so creatively a few feet out in front of you, either slightly to the left or right of center, and know that you have placed it there for your continued use and that only you know where this wand is. (Your wand has your personal frequency attached to it so no one else can see it.)

Once you've made your wand and set it, it's automatic and remains out of view *until it is triggered*. When discordant energy surfaces in your life, your magic wand automatically appears in your field of vision. It's as automatic as the lights coming on in your home when you flip a switch. Practice laser-beaming onto troubling energy. Don't focus on the illusion but "see through" it with intended Love, focused in and conveyed through your wand, your conscious attention.

Do you see? Your wand is your focused conscious "intention" of Love...because that's where the power is.

"Thou sword of truth, fly swift and sure, that evil die and good endure!" - Flora, Sleeping Beauty/Disney

Remember, you are the vibration of Love. That is your authentic frequency. When you are vibrating Love you are authentically aligned with the Power of YOU, your most perfect expression and magic happens!

Don't let your subconscious mind interpret your present situations. Allow your present mind of Love to rule.

All energy is Love in action at its source. When seemingly negative conditions appear in your life, rely on your higher, refined senses. Look with your "inner eyes" beyond what your outer senses are telling you and you will see Love. But you must move beyond any personal opinions into Unity, or you will continue to color and cloud your perceptions.

When your "eyes and ears" have been tuned to Love, seeing and hearing only Unity in all things expressing, then you no longer contribute to the creation of separation by seeing separation.

There is simply no vibration that can resist the power of Love because Love is the single frequency that all things have in common, that all things originate from. It is the point of Unity, the original Source we all share, yet most people simply have no idea that they have this power right within themselves, the power to transmute energy, change their lives and the world around them.

When you consciously transmute lower energy into higher energy by your focused intention of Love (your magic wand), you are exercising your rights as the Master Alchemist that you were born to be. This empowers you and grants you the use of magic.

Remember the great creative commandment... *"Let there be Light."*

Go into a dark room and flip on the light switch. Darkness vanishes. Darkness is nothing more than the absence of light. Likewise, *when you turn on/shed the "Light of conscious understanding/Love," your dark thoughts vanish as Light/Love rules.*

Our once dominant programming of fear is becoming obsolete as the *cycle of suns* ushers in a new day. We are learning to operate from Love.

Remember, you are the Grand Alchemist, shifting energy from low to high, from dark to Light, from fear to Love...*all within you.* You are the instrument the Divine works through to transmute energy and expand the expression of Love eternally. You are the Divine Alchemist if you just claim your powers and make use of them.

....

"The secrets of alchemy exist to transform mortals from a state of suffering and ignorance to a state of enlightenment and bliss."
– Deepak Chopra

....

The Final Frontier

*Quit living for others
and embrace the
beauty of yourself!*

18

In Love with Love

As these new high-powered, DNA shifting photons arrive in this grand time of our entrance into The Age of Aquarius, the embedded "fear" frequencies within us are being stirred up rapidly. They are rising to the surface, so they can be healed and transformed by the intense Love vibration embracing them.

"The wheat is being separated from the chaff." No longer do we have the luxury of wallowing in our negative perceptions.

The quickening is occurring. The Earth is ascending, and if we are to consciously ascend with her to higher dimensions, then these fear/victim energies must be cleared and transmuted into Love.

Are you coming? It's an open invitation, and if you've read this far along, you are likely ready to complete this mission of purifying your mind/consciousness and body to ascend into higher dimensions of Love, Light and Life.

The way is narrow. Falling in Love with Love – falling in Love with YOU – is the final frontier and the only way in. There is no other. *There is one path – to become a servant to Love, to ~~vibrate~~ the resonance of Love, to "be" the resonance of Love.*

You must fall eternally and completely in love *with you* until nothing remains in your energy signature but Love. You must align with and express your authentic self always, manifesting Heaven on Earth, our new Camelot.

To "be" is an action step. Action can only happen in the "now" moment, for the "now" is where magic lives, where creation takes place, and where you dance with your beloved.

"Residing within the journey, not looking at a projection of what that journey might be. You've stopped focusing on the reflections, the shadows in life, when you begin to reside in the moment where the journey happens." Merlin

We must become as children again, living in the moment, without the concept of duality/past and future, with the love and joy of journeying, of experiencing life *now* as it appears before us, without coloring it with preconceived conditions/ perceptions, beliefs, and judgments. *That is the secret.*

Creation never closed itself off to us. We closed ourselves off to creation by living in fear and limitation.

Trusting and being in love with Life, being in love with ourselves in every moment – *being in love with Love* is the simple answer. Don't complicate and confuse things with your defense mechanisms.

There is nothing but Love trying to express Love! We would see that easily if we'd just get out of the way with our personal opinions, harmonize our thoughts with Love, and become servants to Love.

Attaining mastery over our lower nature of fear and consciously expressing our new, higher evolved nature of authentic Love in every moment is what this evolutionary game is about. We cannot love every moment unless we are "seeing," unless our perceptions reflect the Truth of every moment. *Until we see Love in every moment.* We cannot choose Love consciously until we know ourselves as Love and totally, unconditionally "fall in love with ourselves."

We cannot fall in love with ourselves until we KNOW without doubt that *our true nature is divine* (because we always judge anything that appears less than divine) – until our awareness KNOWS, without a doubt, who it is.

Falling in love with ourselves is proof that we know of our Divine Heritage…that we are Divine beings.

Once your frequency is aligned with Love, you generate Light and vibrate at the highest possible human frequency, and no darkness – including death – resonates there.

When you shift your consciousness to a higher frequency, the atomic structure of your body changes because *your body is a vehicle of consciousness and cannot exist without it.*

Joseph Chilton Pearce in "The Biology of Transcendence" states that "Transcendence is our biological imperative, a state we have been moving toward for millennia."

Consciousness is making an evolutionary leap into a higher dimension and clarity of Love. Love can never be bound by time/past or future, by limits, labels, borders, or barriers – nor any personal conceptions of fearful minds. Neither past nor future exist where Love lives, and life expresses. Only the eternal "now" abides there.

Why do you think they call it the "present?" *It's the greatest gift ever given, for it contains the potential for all others.*

When you align your full awareness/resonance with that of Love, your focus is in the now moment, on a moment-to-moment basis. *Since Love expresses as Life, when you align your consciousness with Love, you are resonating with Life and you eliminate death.*

Death has no power when there is nothing left to die. It's just a matter of resonance.

The only way to bring forth the brilliance of your inner crystal, your Divine Spark, is to Light up the darkness until all fear-based thoughts and perceptions within your frequency have been transmuted and you finally recognize the Pure Diamond Crystal of Love that you are and fall deeply and completely in love with yourself. That's the true unconditional love that we're all searching for. *It is the purest and deepest form of Love there is.*

You must be in complete surrender and devotion to Love. A servant in service to Love. Love in love with Love. *You in love with you.*

When you fall in love with yourself with the same purity of Love a mother feels when she first looks into the eyes of her newborn child, then you will have reached the intensity of Love needed to attain Christhood. When you can authentically present yourself at all moments and be totally in love with who you are, it generates a power that cleanses the last residues of ash from your carbon structure to reveal the Pure Radiant Diamond Crystal within you.

When you love yourself with such devotion and acceptance of who Love created you to be, without any limits and judgments, personal opinions or guilt, without wanting to change anything about yourself... there is such Light generated that no darkness remains in your bodily cells. All the dross carbon is burned off as you "switch on the Light of Love." Your Solar-Light (your Soul-Light) beams, and you Light up from within.

This is the moment of complete Union with yourself, when you have fallen in love with YOU.

Your mind has discovered and fallen in love with your heart, and they have become one in the Divine Marriage.

In that moment, you give up your stories and dramas, leave the past behind and the future alone, exit your made-up world of fears and embrace the "present," where *Love expresses as Life eternally.*

You become the pure reflection of the Light of Christ Love because there is nothing left in your consciousness that does not reflect this pure Love. Nothing remains in you to block the Light. You have, *with conscious intent*, dropped all the veils of illusion that formally concealed your radiance. *The dark thoughts, the guilt and judgments you placed on yourself out of fear, have shifted, and the energy is now radiating with Love for who you are.*

As a perfect Diamond Crystal, you are radiantly beautiful and crystalline in nature. You are now a receiver and generator of Light – *a transmitter of Light* – a "Light Being," a "Christed Light Being," a Crystal Light – because nothing stands between you and the Light. Your Diamond Crystal shines forth with its flawless brilliance without distortion or shadow.

This change, this metamorphosis from caterpillar to Cosmic Butterfly, from human to Divine, releasing your inner crystal and expressing Divine Radiance, *is your natural path. It reflects Life* in the same way as metamorphosis from caterpillar to butterfly. It is what you are created to do, and anything less than that is *unnatural and reflects death* the same way the death of a caterpillar before completing its life cycle of becoming a butterfly (it's full potential) is unnatural.

Christ Consciousness is consciousness born of Divine Union, when the passions of the heart are joined with the logic/actions of the mind in Unity of Divine Purpose, on Earth as it is in heaven. It is the highest level of consciousness you can achieve as a human, and the only way you can access this highest portal of thought/expression is through your own human consciousness.

It is human consciousness that evolves into Divine/Christ Consciousness, and the vehicle for human consciousness is your body. Your body is the portal to Divine Consciousness. It is your vehicle for ascension in this lifetime.

Christ consciousness is perfected human consciousness. Human consciousness expresses and evolves through physical form. The physical body is the tool used by Love to evolve consciousness from human to Divine.

Perfected human consciousness is "enlightened" consciousness, one that knows itself as Love and all things as Love and "sees and hears" only Love, always. *It Lights up the darkness with its purity, with its brilliance, with its radiance, with its Love.*

As we evolve as a species, so too does the world around us, because everything is connected. Shifting our consciousness from lower to higher frequencies is what shifts the world around us. *Not the other way around.*

Everyone is perfectly aware of the warmth of Love that is felt when wrapped in the frequency of Love from another. Because of our cosmic alignment, we are currently being hit by an intense wave of Love, photonic Light – Light is Love. It is melting cold, cold hearts.

Reflect on the steam, water, and ice metaphor...What happens to the rock-hard ice when heat is applied? It starts to melt. Keep that heat (Love) coming and ice (fear) is transformed into steam (Love). *We are moving out of fear into Love.* There are no more excuses.

The Physical Body

"The exact process of metamorphosis leading to the creation and birth of the spirit body within the physical body has long been veiled in mystery and secrecy."

– Arion Love

19

The Holy Grail

Since everything expresses as some form/frequency of energy, it follows that your level of vibration – the denseness or Lightness of your thoughts – not only determines what dimension you are *consciously operating from*, but also the amount of Light that is flowing through your "body electric" (your physical body). Higher and lighter-frequency thoughts generate and allow Light to flow (they are *transmitters* of Light), whereas lower, denser, darker thoughts are veils that block the Light, dam the flow and cause shadows.

The physical body is the densest manifestation of consciousness. It came into being as a vehicle to express the Divine in form through the consciousness that animates it.

Without consciousness, the physical body does not exist. The physical body exists because of consciousness. That's why you have a body in the first place.

Therefore, if your consciousness expresses, reflects, and resonates at a very high frequency, that of Love and Light, it would follow that your body (which is integral to your consciousness) would also resonate at the same frequency of Light. Right?

Of course, you can't separate them. When you do, "death" or recycling happens to the dense physical form because it has no reason for "being" without consciousness to animate it, and simply follows the laws of form, "from dust to dust," etc.

Just as everything in the heavens has a Divine purpose and isn't just "hanging out," so too does everything on Earth have a Divine purpose and doesn't just happen.

Your body has a Divine purpose beyond just being recycled.

*Your body is part of the process of evolution...not to be discarded but to be evolved...*a whole different scenario than moving on without a body. You need a 5th dimensional body, one that is woven of Light – of Love consciousness – before you can take the next step up the evolutionary ladder.

"One of the great occult laws is that to function in any sphere or plane of substance in nature you must have a body sensitive to and capable of adjustment with that plane of substance." — Manly P Hall; Magic: A Treatise on Esoteric Ethics

The physical body is the Holy Grail, the Divine Vehicle through which the Immortal Divine Christed Son is realized. It is the vehicle used to integrate light with form, spirit and matter, male and female, heaven and Earth.

You must understand the Divine purpose of the physical body to appreciate and align with this purpose consciously.

The physical body is the vehicle used to evolve consciousness from a low frequency of separation and fear to one vibrating at the highest frequency and Unity of Love. Its sole purpose is to develop a consciousness so aligned with Love that it reflects and radiates only Love in form – the Divine Human.

Everything you presently hide behind, including your beliefs, was created out of fear, when you were trying to protect yourself because you did not yet recognize yourself as Love. We are currently getting tuned to and aligned with the frequency of Love. All fear-driven thoughts/programs and perceptions must be consciously transmuted into Love, the new operating system.

We do this by planting Love where others fear.

Love, by its high/fast vibration, is "Light as consciousness and Life as form." Fear, being the opposite of Love, is low and slow in vibration. It is darkness as consciousness and death in form. Need I say more?

Remember, there is no "if, and, or but" in this new paradigm, so don't start coloring it with logic. There is only one way in, so don't fool yourself into believing you can find another way in or that you can somehow slip in a lower-frequency thought. I admit, it's hard to let go of some of the "protective" mechanisms we've put in place...but we can't ascend with them in tow.

If you don't resonate the high frequency of Love, you can't experience the 5th dimension because you are not really entering anything; you are aligning with and synchronizing vibration/frequency and awareness.

It's really that simple. Until your frequency resonates in complete harmony with Love, you cannot express the fullness of Love…a requirement for the 5th dimension.

So, how do you pass through this narrow entrance, eliminate fear, and resonate fully in the frequency of Love?

The only way to address and remove your fears so that you radiate the fullness of your inner Light is to shift your perceptions, because that's where your fears live. Start paying attention to your thoughts and feelings, observe them, honor them, and own them. Recognize that your fear-based thoughts were put into place as your protectors and release them from their duties. They never meant you any harm; they were just trying to protect you from getting hurt. Don't hate them – love them. *Love and transmute the energy into Love.*

In other words, quit trying to change others and things outside of yourself, and address your own thoughts and issues, the ones that keep you from being authentic, the ones you hide behind and deep within, the ones that keep your thoughts and perceptions outside of Love. Drop whatever shakes your foundation from its natural state of peace.

How many times during the day do you come down on yourself for one reason or another? The next time you find yourself doing that, pause and take a deep breath (one of the quickest ways to clear negativity) and observe what you are feeling. You can trace that feeling to fear, and shift that fear into Love, for you.

Remember, this is all about you. You are working on your personal perceptions and no one else's. To consciously choose Love over fear in every moment empowers you and shifts your programming, your perceptions.

You cannot shift frequency by working on others. (Why would anyone ever believe they have authority to work on others?) You shift frequency by consciously working on yourself, the only authority anyone has. *You have the ability and power to shift your own frequency, to be in control, to become Master of your life.*

That is the magic and the alchemy. It is your great privilege to discover and embrace whatever it is about *you* that needs shifting and realigning with the frequency of Love. It is the only way to change you and the world around you.

Consciousness exists in all dimensions. It is Love expressing as Light. But consciousness of self, or self-awareness CANNOT EXIST WITHOUT A BODY. A body provides the localized electric brain/mind that eventually, after eons of experience and focus without, *turns within, becomes self-aware, and recognizes itself as Love.*

This is the highest perception (program) that a human mind is capable of – to KNOW and express itself as Love, its authentic vibration!

. ...

In ruling one's mind man becomes the Master! And
mastery is the first step beyond mortality.
It opens the doors to divinity.
– Annalee Skarin

The Light-Body

"Where there is love,
there is life."

– Mahatma Gandhi

20

Mortal to Immortal

Your body is the expression of consciousness in form, and conversely, your consciousness is the reflection of your experiences. They work hand in hand, one growing the other. Therefore, *the change in your body from a mortal state to an immortal state is through a change in consciousness.* There is no other way.

These dense mortal bodies that we currently express in are nothing more than a product of our current limited consciousness. As consciousness absorbs Light and rises in frequency, the cells of the body (that house this Light) change at an atomic/molecular level, and this change reflects throughout the body, shifting us from carbon to crystalline in nature, radiant and imperishable.

Like all created things, the body has a divine purpose. It is the vehicle in which to evolve consciousness, with a mind to express this evolved consciousness fully – one in touch with

Divinity. All this happens through lifetimes of experiences that the body (the physical senses) go through, record and file.

Therefore, if your body is an expression of consciousness and your consciousness is fully expressing and aligned with Love, it follows that your body is aligned with and expressing Love also. How could it be otherwise?

When every cell, atom, and subatomic particle of your being has aligned with and resonates Love, that in turn expresses as Light and Life. What has power over that?

When you are fully vibrating with Love, which is Life, where does death get its sting?

It is simply an alignment of frequencies. Love expresses/resonates Life; fear expresses/resonates death.

You are what you resonate. If your frequency expresses only Love, then you are Life itself, and nothing can touch you...including death. If your frequency aligns with fear then you resonate with death and must play by those rules.

The key is to get out of all your fairy tales, the "what if's" and "but maybe's," the voice that is full of excuses and mired in fantasy. The voice that so subtly tries to convince you that you can somehow skirt these rules and hang on to some of your favorite fears, while letting others go. It doesn't work like that. There are laws, structures that hold up the Universe, and everything is subject to these laws.

There is no great being somewhere that is going to look down and take pity on you because of your circumstances and "let you in." *This is a vibration game.* The only thing that matters is what your frequency is, how you are resonating, putting you in full control.

When you strip away all your protective coverings, made-up stories, dramas, and excuses about your life, the only thing left is Love. This is true for all of us.

Physical Immortality is nothing mysterious...it is the natural course of things. It is the result of aligning with and consciously expressing our authentic vibration and highest expression...Love. Death of the physical body is unnatural, it is the by-product of resonating with and expressing fear/dense frequencies.

As consciousness evolves to higher dimensions and expressions of Love, the physical body naturally reflects this "inner growing light" – how could it not? They are connected.

When all bodies – spiritual, mental, emotional, and physical – are synchronized, aligned with and operating as one unit with *one purpose*, consciously in line with Love, the Unity-Verse (the Uni-verse) you are in tune and express pure Light because you have no "shadows of doubt." *Since your body reflects your consciousness, it too expresses pure Divine Light without shadow.*

The process is simple...

You create *by your conscious alignment with Love* a body made of Light, one whose cells are woven from the beautiful threads of Divine Love/Light and Life.

You become LUMINOUS, or maybe I should describe it as your luminosity being released as your blockages are alchemized to Love. Impurities are removed and transmuted, your "lead is changed to gold" and carbon crystallizes into Light as your fears shift into Love.

Light Bodies are the natural result of raising and aligning our consciousness with that of Love, which is Light. It is our most natural course, our highest potential, and the next step in the evolution of mankind.

This newly woven Light Body made of pure Light is also called the Rainbow Body because it reflects all seven colors of the rainbow, or virtues of Divine Love. (All seven major chakras are resonating perfectly and in alignment.) The Light Body has other names as well depending on the culture, religion, or myth you reference. Immortal body, Star Body, Radiant Body, Golden Body, Golden Pearl, and Divine Body are all names associated with the Light Body. In ancient Egypt, it was called the "Luminous Body or Being," and the Taoists called it the "Diamond Body." I'd like to grace it with the name "Cosmic Butterfly."

This Light Body is our vehicle of Love expressing in form as we operate from the conscious awareness of Love, the new "divine system." This is the body we evolve to operate in the 5th dimension, the dimension of Love that we are presently creating on Earth through our conscious alignment with Love.

As you go through your "metamorphosis" stage, clean out, remove, and shift your inner perceptions, command your thoughts to recognize Love (rather than fear) in every moment.

Standing fast in that conviction of Love, your perceptions

(your consciousness) and cells (your physical form) shift to reflect this light.

In other words, you can't sport a "gleaming new consciousness" of sparkling White Light without sporting a "gleaming new body" of sparkling White Light, because the physical form is simply a reflection of consciousness.

Since Love is your true authentic vibration, you have moved into your perfect authentic expression. You are *Love in spirit, Light in consciousness, and Life in form*, the Holy Trinity. Love, Light and Life. Where there is Love, there is Light; where there is Light, there is Life. Where there is Life, there is Love...and the circle of creation goes on forever, worlds without end.

It is the Eternal Flame, expanding the expression of Love eternally.

The process is simple if you are brave enough to let go of all the confusing definitions and explanations you've been fed that do nothing but complicate things.

When your mind/consciousness aligns with Love...*your physical body aligns with Light and expresses Life.*

When your mind/consciousness aligns with fear, your physical body/frequency aligns with darkness and *expresses death.*

Can it get any simpler than that? The higher, finer, and more in harmony your frequency is with your true authentic frequency of Love, the lighter, finer, and more in harmony your cells are with Life, with the Unity-Verse, the Symphony of Love.

The more you are *consciously* aligned with Love, the faster your frequency, and greater is the Light that you generate. *You literally "Light up from within," and nothing – not even death – has power over Light and Life.*

Mortals are mortal by "virtue of" their frequency alignment with fear, which is always temporary and limited.

Immortals are immortal by "virtue of" their frequency alignment with Love, which is always permanent and eternal.

The Eternal Flame

"You are on the verge of birthing a new consciousness. This is a consciousness that has fully released the need to control or possess anything. It is free of fear. It is the Christ consciousness."

— Jeshua

21

The Star That You Are

By the time you have reached this high level of conscious understanding and expression of Love, you will have worked very hard to clean up your personal space and eliminate any thought, feeling, word, or act that is out of alignment with the frequency of Love. You now understand that it is these very thoughts, words, and acts that keep you vibrating at a slow, dense frequency, and in alignment with fear and death.

Was all that conscious cleansing, scrubbing, polishing, cutting, and spit-shining worth it? Was cleaning the subconscious of all its dark fears and consciously transmuting the energy into Love worth your time and effort?

In other words, was the "gain worth the pain?"

You bet it was.

All that purification revealed the Radiant Diamond Crystal within you in all its gleaming and multifaceted splendor. This Crystal is the "star" that you are, your true authentic Self…the Divine Spark of Love that holds the perfect blueprint of you.

It's been hidden under many layers, many veils of illusion (your distorted beliefs etc.) and masks of deception. Every time you presented yourself in a non-authentic way you hid behind a mask and created another illusion.

But this spark, however dim, was always there because you couldn't be you if it weren't.

It's where the magic is.

Just as the potential of carbon is a crystal diamond, the potential of your carbon-based body/consciousness is crystalline/pure diamond in nature too. This Diamond Crystal is you minus all that is false; it is nothing but pure Light/Love…a perfectly faceted Divine Crystal, your "Christ Self."

The problem with vibrating fear (beyond the obvious) is that fear is not your authentic vibration. You are a spark of the Divine Flame of Love, and as such you are the fullness and perfection of Love. *Fear is a false power*…something outside of you that *you empowered,* something you made up for protection when you did not recognize yourself as Love.

God is very stern about honoring another power. You'll recall the first of the Ten Commandments: "I am the Lord thy God; thou shalt have no other Gods before me."

Never put fear before Love…when you do, you are honoring a false God.

As a spark of the Divine Flame of Love, you hold the same properties and potential of the Original Flame, just as a spark off any flame no matter how small, holds the full potential of its parent flame.

However – and this is very important – your true greatness, your true potential, lies not in staying a spark...but becoming a flame.

As a flame, you burst into many sparks, and the circle of life begins again.

As a spark, you give birth to the flame, and as the flame you give birth to sparks.

All sparks have the same potential to become flames, but they must have the appropriate elements at hand to stay lit and continue burning just as your campfire spark must have both oxygen to fuel the burn and something to burn. Without those elements, the fire goes out on its own...it extinguishes itself.

Beginning to sound familiar?

This process works the same for you because everything operates under Universal Laws. You are a spark of Love but cannot grow into a flame without the appropriate elements of focused conscious Love in the present, where Love is found and nurtured. These elements are needed to fuel this flame of Love and keep it lit eternally. *Your conscious focus of Love is the fuel.*

Let me say it again: Your true greatness, your true potential, lies not in staying a spark, but in becoming a flame, to expand the expression cf Love which is Light, to literally *"Light up the darkness with your flame of Love."* Do you see? This spark of you becomes the flame that gives birth to sparks that become flames that give birth to sparks that become flames...and the circle of life goes on for eternity, *worlds without end.*

How powerful is that?

Your authentic frequency (spark) is literally the vibration of Love (remember, you as a spark came from the flame of Love in the circle of life), and when you align your frequency with fear, you are living in discord and distortion of your authentic frequency and honoring a false power. Dis-ease of your mental, emotional, and physical bodies sets in because you are out of alignment/resonance with how you were created to operate...*what your true purpose is.* Just as your car cannot run smoothly and operate effectively when it is out of alignment with its true purpose, neither can you.

Your life becomes a series of shimmies, bumps, bruises, and breakdowns until you realign with your authentic frequency...that of Love.

"Neurons that fire together wire together. You can rewire your brain for higher consciousness by focusing on love."

– Deepak Chopra

....

Let's review the steps that got you to this heightened level of awareness:

Yawn...you wake up. Your consciousness/awareness wakes from a long "Sleeping Beauty" slumber and you discover there is more to life than what you previously *perceived;* you are now aware of not only the outer world, but your inner world/self.

You begin searching deeper in your newfound discovery for life's answers by turning in rather than out. Your focus and attention have shifted inward, and you are now on the journey of self-discovery...of being self-aware, of being self-conscious.

Your inner journey reveals dimensions of yourself you were not acquainted with before, and you discover that *you are awareness itself, expressing in physical form.*

You further discover that the past and future are defined by each person differently...they are nothing but personal perceptions. Strip away all those personal limitations, definitions and perceptions and what are you left with? Love; for *only Love embraces all things without judgment, conditions, or personal definitions.* Love is the Impersonal YOU, your authentic self...stripped of conditions and open to all possibility.

Your journey inward has given you tools to recognize and begin to silence the ever "talkative" mind/voice that is constantly in chatter mode, feeding you solutions to your new present issues with "old" subconscious files. Eager to keep you anxious about a future that never arrives, or lost in a past you can't change, it is *stealing your precious presence.*

(If the mind held the answers to your present problems, you would not be in undesired situations, or experience persistent problems. The mind does not know the answer! The mind is what attracted trouble, so why would you turn to it to get you out?)

Would you use old computer programming to solve your new computer problems? Of course, not, but that's exactly what you do when you use your old subconscious files to solve your present problems rather than listening to your heart/intuition, which operates *now, eternally, in the moment.*

You begin hearing another gentler voice as the "talkative" one is silenced. This is your inner voice/intuition that was previously drowned out by your talkative voice. You discover when you listen and follow directions from your inner voice that your life is peaceful, at ease, and loving. You are synchronized and in the flow of your perfect expression; conversely, when you give your attention to this loud persistent voice, your life becomes confusing, chaotic, and the worst thing ever – *repetitive!*

You discover that *your true authentic vibration is Love and that this gentle inner voice that you've become acquainted with is the voice of Love* speaking through your heart, the original "spark" of you. You have discovered the Holy Grail.

You realize that like most others, you have been approaching life backwards and trying to create from the outside in. You now see that the process works from the inside out and the only way to shift the outside world is to shift your inner world first. You now know that's where the controls are, just as the controls are on the inside of your car. Yes, it's true, there are remote cars that are controlled from the outside...and this is you when you have not taken control on the inside. You are being remotely controlled by outer influences often referred to as "mass consciousness."

You develop *"eyes that see and ears that hear"* by keeping your attention/energy and focus in the present moment where Love lives. Love could never live in the past or future; that's where personal definitions live. Your past and future belong to you alone. They are created from your limited files, but the moment belongs to Love and to everyone equally, because *Love loves all things equally. The moment offers you full potential and all possibility, for full potential can only live where limiting definitions do not.*

You rid your frequency of any vibration/thought/belief/ judgment or guilt (about yourself or others) that is not aligned and resonating with Love in the moment. (Remember, the toughest fears and guilt hidden in the deepest recesses of your mind are all directed at you.) *What remains is a pure uncontaminated resonance/frequency, the Light of Love expressing in physical form, the Mind of Christ…Christ Consciousness.* You begin to sparkle as a perfect crystal diamond as you connect with, reveal, and express your true facets of Love, Praise, Peace, Joy, Harmony, Gratitude, Grace, and Forgiveness in every moment.

This story is all about you and always has been about you because you do not have the authority to change anyone but yourself, and neither does anyone else. The only energy we can shift is our own personal energy, the energy that bears our signature, the energy that we are. It is by shifting our own energy into alignment with Love that we shift others *through our shared frequency connection in Love*…not by trying to change others.

You continue to fall deeply in Love with yourself as you recognize yourself as Love and become "Christed" or "Anointed" (Christ means "Anointed One"). Expressing your Perfect Diamond Crystal (your Christ Consciousness), your physical body (which is an expression of your consciousness in form) transforms naturally from one of dense geometric carbon to one of full silica/crystalline matrix structure…that of Light – *a Light Body, a body made of LIGHT. This is the highest potential and next stage in the evolution of mankind, the marriage of consciousness and form, light and matter, Heaven and Earth.*

Although sounding and appearing mysterious to the non-awakened, this change in the physical body is the natural result of your shift and lift in consciousness. Your Light Body is created from within (not from anything that you or anyone else can do outside yourself). This is an inside job: your mission is to clean up your mind so that it can hold the fullness of Love. And in the process of "conscious cleansing" into Love, your bodily cells (your conscious expression in form) change automatically because *your body is always an expression of your consciousness.*

When your consciousness is comprised of the highest thoughts possible, *the perfect expression and reflection of Love, you express Divine Will on Earth as Christ Consciousness, the purest, highest, and clearest expression of Love in form.*

You are the pure Light of Christ as you receive, accept, and KNOW that you are this Light. You become a receiver and generator…a transmitter of Pure Love/Light/Life through this knowledge, acceptance, and expression.

Your metamorphosis into a Cosmic Butterfly, a Cosmic Light Generator; The Cosmic Christ in action, the Light of Love in form is complete.

You are now free to BE whatever it is your heart desires because you are harmonized and, in the flow, resonating with the fullness of Love, your authentic self.

The Light of Love consciousness and the expression of it in form is the expression of the new human, the Divine Human, the Christed One. *The One who lives in form but expresses consciously the fullness of Love.*

Without definition or distortion. Without restriction, shadows, conditions, and limitations of the personal mind.

Divine Consciousness, expressing in form, gives birth to the Divine Human, Homo Luminous, the Christ.

Fly high,
Cosmic Butterfly

"Weave this purified energy into the Collective Cup of Humanity's Consciousness, so that this precious Life energy will be used by every person's I AM Presence in the Divine Alchemy of transforming our carbon-based cells into the infinite perfection of our 5th-Dimensional Crystalline Solar Light Bodies."

– Patricia Diane Cota-Robles

22

Playground of the YOUniverse

A s you journey from low, slow caterpillar to high-flying Cosmic Butterfly, you learn to observe your every notion and feeling (your use of energy) until there is nothing in your signature that is not aligned and resonating with the frequency of Love.

You come to understand this journey from a higher perspective, as you use your inner eyes and ears to perceive. You realize this is all about YOU, about releasing the made-up versions of you, a process of dropping your veils and coming out from behind your mask. It's about LOVING and BEING your authentic self always, with complete and unconditional acceptance of who you are, *of who Source created you to be.*

Only then can you, with Love, give this complete acceptance/Love/gift to others. *It is your greatest gift to receive and your greatest gift to give.* When you raise your frequency, you raise the frequency of all others because we are all connected through the frequency of Love.

When your frequency expresses nothing but Love, you have graduated to the world of Love, the world of Harmony, in alignment with the "Unity-Verse, the Universe." You have aligned with the Universal Song of Love. You-in-verse, in complete harmony…the Divine Human, the I AM Presence in perfect balanced expression, in perfect form.

Just as Sleeping Beauty was kissed by Love and woke from a long slumber to live happily ever after, so too have you been "kissed" by pure Love (which is authentic Love of self, an alignment of your frequency/thoughts with Love) and given *the gift of living happily ever after.*

Congratulations, and welcome home. You have earned and received your admission to the Playground of the YOUniverse reserved for the pure, innocent, and free mind of a child, where *Magic lives and Love expresses.*

There is a sign on the playground gate and it reads:

Only innocent children allowed.
All problems must be left at the gate.
No baggage allowed in.
Leave excess weight behind.

Go forth, frolic and play for Eternity, for there is no past or future here, there is only the magic moment, the greatest gift you've ever been given, the "Present." It is the Eternal Moment, where All Potential exists for you to express Joy and live "happily ever after."

Only by falling "deeply and completely in love with yourself" and honoring who you are, are you granted the privilege and highest honor of consciously "living forever" ...eternally expressing Love/Light/Life...

It is at this moment of complete Love for yourself, when you *KNOW yourself and everyone else as Love, that you align with Unity* and crack open your chrysalis, which has lovingly served to transform you from low frequency to high frequency, from darkness to Light, from mortal to Immortal.

We are set to take a giant leap in evolutionary status as we move up the frequency scale. The real fun begins as we become conscious participants in this *grand transformation of mankind from mortal to immortal, from human to Divine.*

From caterpillar to butterfly, carbon to crystal, *and fear to Love.*

It's so simple, so natural, and so "now."

. . . .

It's just a matter of frequency. When your consciousness aligns with Love, you are filled with Light and every cell expresses Life. What has power over that?

. . . .

Enlightened Reader...

*S*o, there you have it. Your journey from caterpillar to high-flying Cosmic Butterfly – who knows only Love in every moment, reflects only Light in every moment, and expresses Life in every moment – is complete.

I hope I've helped to connect the dots and brought clarity to your understanding of this Simple Divine Operation of Love, Light, and Life as it has been revealed to me.

There is only ONE story being told, one play being played out, and that story is Love. Each one of us in our own time "blossoms," becoming consciously one with Love. Like the rose, each one as beautiful as the next, we too have our own time of fulfillment.

If you don't take anything away from this book other than a knowledge that this whole story is about You, as Love, then I've done my job.

You are the Holy Grail. The "key" to this whole process has been hidden within you the whole time...right under your nose.

This is my Truth as I know it to BE through years of study and expression of Love in my own Life. I am not proselyting. I am simply sharing what I know to be Truth, my story as a guide for you to follow, a resource to turn to...if you choose to, if you resonate with it.

The only real "truth" is your Truth and your comprehension of Truth. No one can give you Truth. It is the gift you give to yourself through your desire and passion to Know Truth. Truth comes from within, it must be gleaned through your own perceptions and no one else's.

In the end, there is only one voice that needs following, one choice that is the perfect expression for you or for me in the moment, and the only access to that voice, that choice, is conscious alignment with Love in the moment.

From fear to Freedom...from blindness to sight...I am ecstatic to be sharing this journey through Eternity with you.

In Love with Love...

Kathy

Works Cited

3.13.7, Chandogya Upanishad. *Aquarian Path.* http://www.aquarianpath.com/mysticalheart.php. 2014.

Achad, Frater. *The Anatomy of the Body of God.* Chicago Illinois: Collegium ad Spiritum Sanctum, n.d. http://hermetic.com/achad/pdf/anatomy.pdf.

Aquarian Age Community. *Aquarian Age Community.* http://www.aquaac.org/dl/99nl4art2.html. 2014.

Bailey, Alice A. *A Treatise on Cosmic Fire.* Lucis Trust, Original version. 1925. http://www.lucistrust.org:8081/obooks/?q=node/290.

— *Sacred Texts.* n.d. http://www.sacred-texts.com/eso/ihas/ihas13.htm. 2015.

Bjorn Carey Staff. *Space.* http://www.space.com/2157-cosmic-dna-double-helix-spotted-space.html. 2013.

Browning, Robert. *Goodreads.* http://www.goodreads.com/quotes/13981-love-is-the-energy-of-life. 2013

Cannon, Dolores. *What Is Quantum Healing Hypnosis Technique?* http://www.dolorescannon.com/about-qhht. 2013.

Cayce, Edgar. *Divine Cosmos.* 2014. https://www.divinecosmos.com/start-here/books-free-online/18-the-shift-of-the-ages/71-the-shift-of-the-ages-chapter-15-cayce-and-ra-speak-on-the-great-solar-cycle. 2014.

Chopra, Deepak. *3tags.org*. http://3tags.org/article/ neurons-that-fire-together-wire-together. 2014.

Chopra, Deepak. The Way of the Wizard: Twenty Spiritual Lessons for Creating the Life You Want. https:// www.goodreads.com/work/quotes/66730-the-way-of-the- wizard-twenty-spiritual-lessons-for-creating-the-life-you

Connolly, Timothy. *Shift of the Age*. http://www. shiftoftheage.com/2009/11/02/precession-of-the-equinox- from-darkness-into-light-2/. 2014.

Cota-Robles, Patricia. *Era of Peace*. 2 February 2014. http://www.eraofpeace.org/blog/index/ list/?dir=asc&order=created_time&p=107. 2015.

Cruttenden, Walter. Patino, Geoff. *The Great Year (A Yuga Project Film)*. 2003. http://www.thegreatyear.com/ thegreatyear/tgy_facts.shtml. 2014.

Crystal, Ellie. *Crystalinks*. http://www.crystalinks.com/ mayancalendar.html. 2014.

Curtiss, Dr. and Mrs. F. Homer. *The Inner Radiance*. Johannesburg, South Africa: Mount Linden Publishing, 1935. http://www.orderofchristianmystics.co.za/pdf/ Curtiss%20FH%20and%20HA%20The%20Inner%20 Radiance%202012%20e-book.pdf.

Dimension, The Fifth. "The Age of Aquarius" or "Let the Sunshine In." Music by Galt MacDermot and lyrics by James Rado and Gerome Ragni. 1969. http://www. metrolyrics.com/aquarius-lyrics-5th-dimension.html.

Disney Film. "Sleeping Beauty" quote. *Disney Magic Quotes*. http://disneymagicquotes.tumblr.com/page/26. 2013

Einstein, Albert. Reflections on Einstein's *The Nature of Life and Dimensions on Earth* - Part 2/2. *Golden Age of Gaia*. n.d. http://goldenageofgaia.com/spiritual-essays/dimensionality/albert-einstein-the-nature-of-life-and-dimensions-on-earth-part-12/. 2014.

— *Quote Investigator*. http://quoteinvestigator.com/2013/09/18/intuitive-mind/. 2013.

Emerson, Ralph Waldo. *Goodreads*. n.d. http://www.goodreads.com/quotes/472078-the-sun-shines-and-warms-and-lights-us-and-we. 2014.

Fiorenza, Nick Anthony. *The Lunar Planner*. http://www.lunarplanner.com/HolyCross.html. 2015.

Friedman, Debbie. *Cleaning Out the Closet of Your Mind*. http://www.cleaningoutthecloset.com/. 2013.

Fukuoka, Masanobu. *Shift of the Age*. 2009. https://shiftoftheage.wordpress.com/2009/11/02/precession-of-the-equinox-from-darkness-into-light-2/. 2014.

Gorgo, Lauren C. *Causal to Conscious Creation*. New York, NY: Expect Miracles, Inc., 2013. http://thinkwithyourheart.com/products/causal-to-conscious-creation

Hall, Manly P. Magic: A Treatise on Esoteric Ethics. https://gnosticwarrior.com/quotes-on-alchemy.html

Harper, John Jay. *Reality Sandwich*. http://realitysandwich.com/23542/suns_god_orion_revelation/. 2015.

Jasmuheen. http://in5d.com/12-stages-of-light-body-ascension/

Jenkins, Dawn Abel quoting John Major Jenkins. *The Message of the Stargates.* http://www.bibliotecapleyades. net/stargate/stargate04.htm. 2014.

Jeshua, Pamela Kribbe channeling *Jeshua.* http:// www.jeshua.net/lightworker/jeshua5.htm. 2014.

Jordan, Pascual. *Information Philosopher..* http://www.informationphilosopher.com/solutions/ scientists/jordan/. 2014.

Lie, Suzanne, Ph.D. *Multidimensions.* http://www.multidimensions.com/multidimensional-consciousness. 2013.

Lloyd, Dr. Janni. *Physical Immortality - The Mass Possibility blog.* https://physicalimmortalitythemasspossibility.wordpress. com/physical-immortality-the-mass-possibility-by-dr-janni-lloyd/. 2014. *"The Fun Way of Physical Immortality Philosophy"*

Love, Arion. *"Alchemy" The Science of Enlightenment.* Kihei, HI, USA 96753: Alchemy Research, 2007. Ebook.

Luckman, Sol. *Conscious Healing.* Bangor, ME: Booklocker Publishing, 2006. http://assets.booklocker.com/ pdfs/2277trial.pdf.

Luna, Barca de. *For Those with Eyes to See.* http:// forthosewitheyestosee.blogspot.com/2013/11/the-answer-lies-within.html. 2013.

Nelson, Ruby. *The Door of Everything.* Camarillo CA: DeVorss & Company, 1963.

http://liberatingdivineconsciousness.com/happiness-is-download-page/.

Oldenkamp, Jacqueline Tull and Johan. *Astrotheology and How to Know Thyself (A Summary of the lectures of Santos Bonacci)*. Pateo Academia, 2012. http://www.pateo.nl/PDF/Astrotheology_summary.pdf.

Osho. Gautama Buddha (credit to. n.d. http://www.lifetrainings.com/Why-the-Law-of-Attraction-doesnt-work.html. 2014.

Rota, Miriandra. *Pretty Flower*. http://www.prettyflower.us/. 2012. https://miriandra.com/merlins-six-part-seminar/All Merlin quotes attributed to Miriandra's channeling of Merlin.

Rumi. Beliefnet. http://www.beliefnet.com/Quotes/Relationships/R/Rumi/Your-task-is-not.aspx. 2013.

Saliba, Mark. *Next Dimension Healing*. Next Dimension Healing 2012.

— *Next Dimension Healing*. n.d. http://nextdimensionhealing.com.au/blog/. 2014.

Shakespeare, William. *Brainy Quotes*. http://www.brainyquote.com/quotes/quotes/w/williamsha382718.html. 2015.

— *SearchQuotes*. n.d. http://www.searchquotes.com/quotation/It_is_the_stars,_The_stars_above_us,_govern_our_conditions./211846/. 2014.

Shockley, Paul. Introduction by Iebele Abel. *The Cosmic Laws of Cosmic Awareness*. Olympia USA: Elmtree & Waters, n.d. http://www.iebele.nl/CosmicLaws.pdf.

Skarin, Annalee. Book of Books, Devorss and Co.

Tones, Healing. Anthony, *Healing Tones blog post.*. http://healingtones.org/2012/05/26/dawn-of-a-golden-age-apotheosis-and-the-rainbow-body/. 2014

Swami Nityananda Saraswati. Solar Nutrition http://www.livingtolive.com/solar.html

Waters, Owen K. *Peace in Practice.* http://www.peaceinpractice.iinet.net.au/ dimensionsofconsciousness.htm. 2015.

Weor, Samael Aun. *Gnostic Teachings.* n.d. http://gnosticteachings.org/the-teachings-of-gnosis/ introductory-information/1719-the-mantra-of-christ-om-manipadme-hum.html?tmpl=component&type=raw. 2015.

Wiki, Bible quote from. *Westwing.wikia.* http://westwing.wikia.com/wiki/The_Ten_ Commandments. 2015.

Wilcock, David. "The Hero's Journey and Precession of the Equinoxes." Laurent Puechguirbal. https://www.youtube.com/watch?v=E0OvRFdOqro.

Zohar, Danah. *End Game Times*; The Awakening http://endgametime.wordpress.com/the-awakening-quantum-mechanics-of-the-human-brain-and-consciousness/. 2014.

About the Author

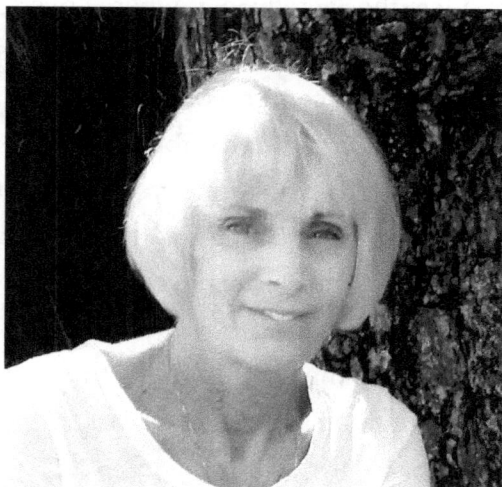

Kathy Dobson is a recognized writer, mystic, spiritual intuitive and pioneer of sacred Truth Principles and Universal Laws. She experienced a deeply mystical awakening in 1976, an electrified "flash of light," shifted her consciousness and opened her eyes and ears to the Truth of physical immortality and Eternal Life, setting her firmly and passionately on the path of enlightenment, self-knowledge and human transformation.

As a humble recipient of these advanced Ascension Laws of Love, Light and Life, it is her mission to fan and spark this sacred flame and awaken humanity to their highest human potential, that of Christ Consciousness, a self-realized God, empowered to create heaven on earth. In 2012 she was touched by another mystical experience that led to the penning of "Consciously Creating Camelot - The Body's Journey to Immortality and the Birth of the Divine Human." Inspired by Master Merlin, these powerful teachings reveal the simple and direct path to the Sacred Heart where Love and Eternity abide and divine alchemy and magic play. Kathy is the owner of PhysicallyImmortal.com, an online resource of shared, consciousness expanding material for all who seek to answer the higher calling of their heart, leave the transitory world of the mundane and enter the eternal world of magic.

These teachings reach far beyond self-improvement, they open the door to self-mastery, bodily translation and human initiation into the Divine. They attract all those who won't settle for anything but the highest service and greatest love.

*"In short, there's simply not
A more congenial spot
For happily-ever-aftering
Than here in Camelot."*

www.ingramcontent.com/pod-product-compliance
Lightning Source LLC
LaVergne TN
LVHW051627080426
835511LV00016B/2216